Under Construction is a true story of courage and resilience. Written by a woman who chases her dreams no matter what obstacles get in the way, Julia keeps constructing her vision as she learns how to build the kind of life she wants to live. Brilliance in progress. I highly recommend reading her story.

Sean Daley

Slug, of the hip hop duo Atmosphere

A page turner, *Under Construction* draws you in with adventure and drama as we witness the courage of the author as she stands in the power of "YES"— the core philosophy guiding her life. Fun and exciting, *Under Construction* will leave you inspired as you root for the author to overcome the obstacles and hurdles, she faces in her life.

Maureen Ryan Blake

Founder of The Power of the Tribe Network
https://thepowerofthetribe.com

This insightful and inspiring story of self-healing and the triumphant spirit of the evolving soul draws you in with its rich storytelling. Both relatable and empowering, Julia Anderson courageously tells the story of the recovery of her shattered self after enduring a heinous attack and takes the reader along as she uncovers the everlasting presence of her creative soul.

Aeriol Ascher, MsD

Author, Empowerment Leader, Coach

UNDER
CONSTRUCTION

*Healing Trauma While
Building My Dream*

JULIA HARRIET

Under Construction
Healing Trauma While Building My Dream
Julia Harriet
Joist Publishing

Published by Joist Publishing, Vashon Island, WA
Copyright ©2021 Julia Harriet
All rights reserved.

Editor: Karen L. Tucker, commaqueenediting.com
Cover and Interior Design: DavisCreative.com

Library of Congress Cataloging-in-Publication Data

Library of Congress Control Number: 2021916236

Julia Harriet

Under Construction: Healing Trauma While Bulding My Dream

ISBN: 978-1-7377243-0-8 (paperback)
       978-1-7377243-1-5 (ebook)

BISAC Subject Headings:
1. SEL021000 SELF-HELP / Motivational & Inspirational 2. SEL016000 SELF-HELP / Personal Growth / Happiness 3. SEL000000 SELF-HELP / General
2021

ATTENTION CORPORATIONS, UNIVERSITIES, COLLEGES AND PROFESSIONAL ORGANIZATIONS: Quantity discounts are available on bulk purchases of this book for educational, gift purposes, or as premiums for increasing magazine subscriptions or renewals. Special books or book excerpts can also be created to fit specific needs. For information, please contact Julia Harriet, Joist Publishing, Julia.harriet@gmail.com, juliaharriet.com

DEDICATION

Dearest Mirabelle and Dockton,

I want to share with you the greatest secret of the universe. It begins within you. You are the universe. Nothing exists outside of you. Which is not to say there isn't incredible magic, mystery, and mountains for you to seek and explore. But first you must find that precious compass inside your heart. That's where your road map lives, where you will find your passion, your pathway, and your purpose. A treasure trove overflowing for your pleasure and fulfillment awaits.

Begin by diving deep inside yourself. Once you find your center, listen to your heart song. Listen to it until a doorway appears. Go and open it. There is only one way through. One truth. One love. One opening of your brilliance. And there You are, in a beautiful, living heaven. It is as much you as you are it. Anything is possible. Everywhere is possible. Imagine. *Imagine!* Feel it in your soul, in the marrow of your bones, and in the pulse of your blood.

You will do great things because you have great hearts. Never doubt that. You were born to do incredible things. To help many people. To love. To be love. To be. You were born to be, and that is enough.

Thank you for inviting me to birth you into this lifetime. Together we are. Thank you.

Dockton and Mirabelle, Point Robinson,
with lighthouse keeper's quarters behind, fall 2016.

TABLE OF CONTENTS

Prologue: Darkness.. 1

The Fortune Teller 5

Chapter 1: The Lighthouse... 9

Into the Deep 15

Chapter 2: Discovery 17

Chapter 3: Adulting 25

Chapter 4: Flower Peddler of Vashon 29

Chapter 5: The Big Questions 33

Chapter 6: The Last Hurrah 39

Chapter 7: The Art of Deconstruction........................ 43

Chapter 8: Open Doors 47

Chapter 9: Builder Buddy for Life 51

Mom and Springsteen 57

Chapter 10: The Good, the Bad, and the Shit 61

Chapter 11: Mourning Tide 65

Mom's Ashes 71

Chapter 12: The Dream Team 73

Chapter 13: Economy of Motion 81

Chapter 14: The Foundation 85

Chapter 15: The Assault 89

Chapter 16: The Monday After................................. 95

Snow White 101

Chapter 17: Trumped... 105

Chapter 18: Hilary the Healer................................. 109

Chapter 19: No Justice, No Peace? 113

Troll Dolls 121

Chapter 20: The Confrontation................................ 123

Chapter 21: The Ridge Beam.................................... 129

Chapter 22: Teen Triumph....................................... 133

Chapter 23: Coming Home 139

Wisdom and Folly...................................... 143

PROLOGUE

Darkness

When I opened my eyes, I was in a bed. Naked. There was a man sleeping next to me. A shadowed stranger. My body felt frozen. I blinked. In excruciating pain, I blinked more. I remained perfectly still. Air lifted my chest. I was alive. My shoulder throbbed. *Would I ever see or hold my kids again?* All I could sense was terror. All I could do was blink.

The man moved. I considered running out the only door, but I didn't know where I was or why I was here. It was as though I had been unplugged and plugged back into a foreign reality.

A large television showed the time: 5:37 a.m. I looked at the man. I had never seen him before. I remembered being outside at the art center but nothing after that. How was that even possible? It didn't matter. I wanted my life more than knowing that answer. I had to live through this moment before I could begin to understand the horrible darkness that mangled my mind.

I slid to the floor in search of my pants, purse, anything that was mine. I could barely swallow. It felt as though something had been wrapped tightly around my neck. I reluctantly coughed, trying to clear the constriction in my throat.

He sat up. "You OK?" he asked.

"I need to get home," I pleaded. "I don't know why I'm here." Our eyes met, though I struggled to focus. I knew I was in danger. I found my pants in the corner of the room, and all five buttonholes had been torn through.

"I know where your car is. I can bring you there now," he said. He could do anything to me, even kill me. But my only hope was to beg for his help. He was my way back home. "Yes. Please get me to my car."

I trembled violently in the passenger seat of his older SUV. Looking out the window, I recognized the neighborhood we were in. I felt momentary relief.

He didn't talk.

My head throbbed with pain. I shut my eyes, but the darkness scared me. I was surrounded by a nightmare. I prayed he wouldn't kill me. I pictured my kids' faces. And my dad. I imagined my dad at my house thinking I am dead. I wanted to live more than I ever had. *Please let me live.*

"I'm so sorry. I really don't know what happened." I hoped that if I took the blame, it might distract him from hurting me further.

"Don't worry about it." He smiled.

"Thank you," I said, "thank you so much for getting me to my car." I was ready to kill him if I had to, but I just kept thanking him, believing my gratitude was drawing me closer to my chances of getting home.

He took me to where my car was parked, a mile or so from the art center in town. I wondered how my car had gotten there.

With my keys in hand, I thanked him once again and shut his heavy car door. I stood outside my car, watching him drive away. Shaking wildly, I finally unlocked my car and collapsed into the driver's seat. I relocked the door, wanting to feel like I was finally safe. My phone rested in the center console. I grabbed it, witnessing the screen overflowing with missed calls and texts. I called my dad. He was sobbing. "I'm coming home, Dad. I'm coming home right now. I'm so sorry. I'm coming home."

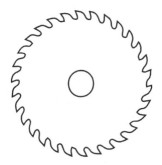

THE FORTUNE TELLER

As a curious 3-year-old, having a world-renowned fortune teller as a neighbor was fantastic. Rose, nestled in a dilapidated white cottage adjacent to our house, smoked constantly, swore in a thick Romanian accent, and had traversed the world selling fortunes to wise men and fools alike.

I would creep off the back porch of my house and scamper across the yard to her door. "Rose, Rose, you home?" I could hear her throw her hefty cat to the carpeted floor.

"Come on now, do come in."

My tight curls stood on end every time I entered her lair of ancient texts, small animal skulls, and black satin.

"Julia, you little precious, come here and let me see you." I entered like it was a sacred tomb. Cautiously intrigued. Ready to run.

Rose would inhale deeply from a long cigarette and hold it, blowing it out as she spoke. "Julia, I have something for you. Something from so far away you can't even picture it in your mind."

I had been given special things like dolls, trucks, books, dresses, but...

"This is a very special someone. See it? This monkey. A monkey of luck. Of wisdom; a maker of the mischief."

Rose handed me a chipped ceramic monkey with faded brown paint. His expression was solemn. Centuries serious. Nothing like the monkeys I had seen at the zoo.

"See the slot here? Look into now."

I did. It was pure darkness inside.

"What you see, sweet Julia?"

I hesitated. My eyes darted down and up, searching for the right answer.

"It's OK," she said. "It's a fucking dark hole." She burst out laughing, startling me, but I smiled, a toothy smile.

"You see this, a money bank. Very old from Europe."

Relief. *OK, this freaky monkey is a good thing.*

"You have a good life, Julia. Understand?"

I'm OK, the monkey is a friend, and Rose says I have a good life. Got it.

"Yes."

She took another long drag and looked upward. "You a special girl. A chosen one. Take the monkey, take it with you. It watch over you. It see much and be friend to you. Keep monkey, yes?"

I held it cautiously in both hands as if it might bite. "Yes. Thank you. I will come back soon, Rose. Bye now."

I walked outside cradling the creepy-looking monkey. It was dusty and had a chipped right ear. "I will have a good life. Yes, I will." I repeated that several times on my way home. A good fortune for a girl to carry.

Rose's ceramic monkey. Held by Mirabelle, 2021.

1. THE LIGHTHOUSE

Lighthouses don't go running all over an island looking for boats to save; they just stand there shining.

- Anne Lamott

Under construction. Like that new school being built down the street. My friend's website. A 35-year-old woman named Julia Harriet (that's me). I hadn't considered myself a builder, although I'd known for a while that my life was one crazy project. Then I realized we are all builders, all constructing our own realities with unique toolboxes filled with things we utilize in living, loving, and being. Rarely do we construct our realities solo—we have partners, allies, and builder buddies that give our lives meaning and depth.

If you've ever been to a job site, you know how messy it is. The garbage is an essential byproduct of the process involved in putting something together. Life is that way too. The crap is unavoidable. But it's what we do with our mess that matters. That's what this story is about: learning how to build with and out from the debris of living. A grand repurposing of trash into treasure. Like any waste product, it won't turn itself into gold. We must rise up and become the alchemists of this transformative process. Otherwise, we'll end up sitting atop piles of our own shit.

A major part of my life's remodel began in early 2015. I was working at an organic daycare in Portland, Oregon, that believed kids had the right to bite because they were exerting their self-will. My wake-up call occurred the day an angry child's teeth penetrated my forearm and I realized teaching preschool was not my jam. But I didn't know what else to do for work given our family's tight schedule and wanting to spend time with my own kids.

My husband, Jake, was a bartender by trade. He took on the day shift of caring for our kids while I taught and then left shortly before dinner to sling drinks until the early-morning hours. It helped us avoid the financial burden of childcare but did a number on our relationship. Tag-team parenting resulted in very little face time with one another, and weeks would pass with only brief strategic check-ins and early-morning rendezvous.

Most evenings, I was at home with Mirabelle, my 5-year-old daughter, and Dockton, my 2-year-old son, making dinner, giving baths, and reading books after a full day of wrangling preschoolers. By my kids' bedtime, I was fucking fried. I would pour myself the largest glass of wine possible and hop on my laptop to perform mindless internet searches—not for stuff to buy or to watch the latest Netflix show; my searches were for alternate realities.

Maybe it was the wine, or the fact I had only eaten my kids' untouched vegetables and called it dinner, but one lonely winter night, I searched for a new life and it responded back. A Google search would end up taking me back to the magical island where I had grown up. This oasis outside of Seattle, Washington, called Vashon, was where rebellious pigs caused traffic issues, and the organic farms outnumbered the restaurants in town. As a child, I rode my bike to the beach most summer days and dropped in on neighbors for cookies and stories. I secretly wanted this idyllic life for my kids but couldn't imagine being able to afford moving back, much less leaving our relatively stable city life.

That January night out in cyberspace, I entered "Jobs on Vashon" in the search bar. It wasn't random. I'd known for a while that I didn't want to raise my kids in Portland, in artificial playgrounds or in friendships they called play-dates that resembled online dating. But because of our jobs, it didn't make sense to move, especially to somewhere that had rental prices resembling San Francisco's.

"Seriously, Julia," I said aloud in a snarky tone, "no one ever gets a job this way, and certainly not on Vashon."

Silence. OK. No. It wasn't likely. But I knew in my heart it was time to light an emergency flare in my life and my marriage, and I had to start somewhere. Nothing came up until several links down. I looked at it in disbelief. There was a caretaker position for the 100-year-old light-house on the island. No way. I had struck gold.

It wasn't a full-time job, but the offer included living in a 550-square-foot apartment in an old WWII coast guard barrack. Damn, it would be so sexy to move back to my hometown as the new family of the lighthouse. Ernest Hemingway, eat your heart out. I drank more wine. This was too romantic to pass up. So, I penned the best love letter to the job post I could muster and then hit send without so much as telling a soul.

When I woke up in the morning, I had a reply in my inbox. The subject read, "Can you come to the island tomorrow to interview?"

I responded instantly in favor of coming then began practicing my pitch to Jake because he would soon wake up to care for the kids. I made him coffee and approached our bed.

"Babe, I have exciting news." I figured I'd just jump right into the deep end.

"I applied to have our family become the new care-takers of the lighthouse on Vashon, and they want to interview us tomorrow."

He took the coffee from me and took a big sip. Looking me in the eyes, he responded with a smile, "Of course you did. What time do we have to be there?"

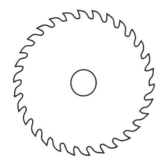

INTO THE DEEP

I tugged my purple coat over my warmest pajamas. The netherworld beneath an old grove of gnarled fir was calling out beyond the cut grass of our tamed yard. Affectionately known as the "Deep Dark Woods," this nocturnal vaudeville housed a ravenous barred owl that my dad had been observing for months.

Pouring himself a generous glass of scotch, my dad swept the tumbler into one hand and took my small, sweaty hand firmly in his other. I held fast to his thick palm, knowing that he was my only beacon in that sea of darkness. Haunting shadows and menacing sounds sparked my imagination's playground as we ventured further from our well-lit home and deeper into the woods.

There were rules of engagement for explorers of the night. Silence was the mandate, with an occasional inquisitive whisper reluctantly accepted. We crept stealthily beneath giant pine boughs.

"Don't move, kid."

I held my breath until I was sure I was turning the color of my winter jacket. I strained to see, but layers of misty darkness obscured the clarity of form. I buried my curly head into my dad's leg and felt prickly petrified, as only a 5-year-old can.

Slicing through the shadows, visible only as a movement, the magnificent creature swept over our heads. We dropped to the forest floor then heard a desperate squeal as the bird lifted its prey back to the branches above.

Paralyzed with shock and amazement, I felt Dad squeeze my hand twice, which meant it was time to return. As we tiptoed between tangles of underbrush, the glow of civilization returned, as did color to my face. I tugged for him to bend down to meet my frozen cheek.

"When can we do it again, Daddy? I want to go back into the Deep."

2. DISCOVERY

And once the storm is over, you won't remember how
you made it through, how you managed to survive. You
won't even be sure whether the storm is really over. But
one thing is certain. When you come out of the storm, you
won't be the same person who walked in. That's what this
storm's all about.

- Haruki Murakami

Doc, Mirabelle, Jake, and I moved to Vashon on a stormy February day in 2015. How could we not? Upon seeing the apartment two weeks prior, as small and shabby as it was, it was obviously our golden ticket to Vashon. A way back home for me. A way to create a more authentic life for us all.

There was inherent risk involved—a family of four sailing away from our structured city life, complete with careers, housing, and 24-hour grocery stores to anchor in 14 acres of wilderness, our only job that of caretaker, with temporary housing in a one-bedroom apartment. But if we didn't go, Jake and I acknowledged we would be haunted by the wonderment of "what if" for the rest of our lives, so we floated ashore with our truck full of belongings to stake our claim on the island.

This profound change in lifestyle quickly exposed unpatchable holes in the hull of my relationship with Jake, and his with me. We had boarded our marital ship in 2011, with hopes of charting open seas and starry skies, but once we left shore, major problems began to surface. We tried to plug them with promises of self-work and less anger-infused outbursts after our kids were asleep. But between caring for children and launching two careers, we burned the candle at both ends. I had hoped that moving to Vashon would give us more community support and time to invest in each other. Instead, as we started spending more time together than ever before in a 550-square-foot apartment, our life change exacerbated our weaknesses, and we were officially lost at sea.

Jake started making plans to move out by fall of 2015, and we became unofficially separated at that time. I "got" the irony of living next to a lighthouse during this hurricane-level transition. Every morning, I awoke to the flashing beacon of light that helped giant container ships navigate the narrow passage safely into the Port of Tacoma. The formidable 100-year-old tower offered me solace as well. Entering the unknown, I knew there would be light to guide my return. I didn't realize, however, how overwhelming the pending storm would become.

Storm approaching from the north,
Point Robinson Lighthouse, 2015.

My mom had been battling colon cancer for a couple of years and seemed to be trucking along until she got a routine CT scan that showed a whole rat's nest in her lungs. She had been a lifelong smoker, yet somehow no one had given her a chest X-ray during her previous treatments. The prognosis was grim. My mom, my best friend, was given a 15 percent chance of survival.

Thanksgiving was fast approaching. I felt like screaming bloody murder into the wind. My husband was leaving me. My mom now too. And in order to spend time with her and travel to Oregon where my parents lived, there was no way I could continue teaching at the middle school, even though I had only begun working there at the start of the school year. This meant that, at least for now, my professional livelihood of the past 10 years in education was ending too.

Since I had only been working at the middle school for a few months when the storm blew in, I had to figure out a way to leave without hurting the students with whom I was privileged to be building relationships. All fourteen of my students were native Spanish speakers, and after our first lesson, one thing had been apparent: they believed school sucked.

About 15 minutes into my first class with them, a student had asked, "Ms. A., why do you think we should give a shit about this stuff?" He paused long enough to gather a round of laughter from the group. "Everyone in this school thinks we're dumb. And that's why we're in your class. Because we don't matter." Some kids snickered while others fell silent.

They all looked at me, hungry for a response. My cheeks flushed. I looked over at the white board covered in words I had written and responded, "Your voice matters to me. That's why! Each of you has a story.

Each of you has dreams and needs. I want to help you communicate them."

What happened next was a mixture of divine luck and a teachable moment of giving zero fucks about the educational system. I knew how broken, racist, and inequitable it was. I knew the kids were right. They had been beaten down and ignored. So, I took my dry erase marker and scribbled wildly all over the neat lecture notes I had written.

"Screw this. You're right. This school disrespects your smarts, and as it is now, it's a waste of your time. Each of you is smart, by the way. And if you've never had a teacher tell you that, then I'm truly sorry."

I could tell the class wasn't sure if I had totally lost my mind, was setting them up for some sort of punishment, or was possibly a cool lady.

"Here's what we are going to do. Let's brainstorm ideas to make this class a better use of your time. What do you want our class time to look like?"

To build trust, I knew I would need to model their answer to the question I was asking. That was fine. I didn't know what that looked like, but I did know I wasn't going to teach these kids the way the class outline required. I was going rogue.

"I want to get to know more about each of you. One of my questions is what kind of activities do you want out here on the island for people your age? I grew up here too, and there wasn't much to do, other than drinking booze and playing video games. My guess is that hasn't changed much."

Heads bobbed in agreement, and a few tales were tossed around about recent debauchery. Then the students dug in and started to talk with one another about their ideas. I stood at the front of the class capturing what I could: bowling; dancing; food trucks; free food—lots of good, free food; homework help; a waterslide park; chill places to hang out after school that were cool.

"Hey, Ms. A., I've been to a place called O Space that does something cool. It's an all-ages dance club. We call it Club O. There's a DJ and food. It goes late, like until 11:00 p.m. They have music and art stuff all year round."

Huh? How had I never heard of this O Space? Cool!

"That sounds like fun. Has anyone else been to O Space?"

Some kids nodded; others looked curious. I gathered from the banter that the full name of the place was Open Space and that it was an art center.

"I have an idea. What if each of you writes a letter to O Space with your wish list of things you want them to offer people your age?"

Enthusiasm percolated. Mistrust did as well.

"How will our letters make a difference?"

"What if they don't even read them?"

I heard one student mumble, "I can't even write a fucking letter."

I paused because I knew my response would make or break everything with them. "I will take your letters personally to the director and read them out loud if I have to. I promise. And I will help each of you write the best damn letter of your life."

Never mind that I didn't know what O Space was before this conversation or who the director was. What I did know was that, no matter what, I would honor this promise. And I made it clear that anything could be asked for within appropriate bounds, but that nothing could be guaranteed.

"Will you give this a try? Give me a thumbs-up if you are willing to try?" I looked around, and at first, I had about 30 percent buy-in. But when the student who had originally called BS on my lesson popped his thumb up, I went to 90 percent within 15 seconds. It was a major breakthrough, one that changed all of our lives forever.

"But one thing, Ms. A. If we actually all do this, can we earn a reward like a pizza party?"

"Oh, hell yes," I said, "but what do you want? A pizza party or something more fun?"

"Ms. Anderson, can we earn bacon-covered brownies if we finish writing our letters to O Space?" Everyone cheered. I had never made bacon into a dessert before, but for this group of seventh and eighth graders who were on the verge of failing or dropping out of school, I would break my meat-to-sweet etiquette to keep them reading and writing.

"Bacon-covered brownies it is. Now let's get to work."

3. ADULTING

Authenticity is a collection of choices that we have
to make every day. It's about the choice to show up
and be real. The choice to be honest. The choice to let
our true selves be seen.

- Brené Brown

At dusk every day, I had to close the gate to the lighthouse. One brisk night in October, I was securing the lock
at the gate and a car pulled up.

"Excuse me, ma'am, are you the keeper of
the lighthouse?"

"Yep, I sure am. Can I help you?

"Well, that's about the coolest job ever. How in the
world does a person apply for that position?"

"It's a long story. But it is pretty amazing living here.
I guess I must be doing something right."

We both chuckled, and the man drove away, real-
izing the park was closed. As I walked back to my house,
I smiled proudly. How in the hell did I end up the caretaker of a lighthouse? At 35, here I was, a single mom,

about to quit teaching for uncharted waters, living next to a 100-year-old lighthouse with her kids.

Honestly, I wasn't sure what I was anymore. As a rule-following good girl, I thought my life would have grown legs and stood more stable by my mid-30s. But instead, it resembled that of a fish swimming in heavy current, constantly moving and adjusting to the flow. My long-held belief of "adulting" was the act of acquiring a husband, holding down a career, maintaining financial security, and owning a home. Sort of like a well-played game of Monopoly. But here I was standing in the muddled center of my midlife remodel, building without a blueprint to follow, lacking most of those things I once strived for.

Adulting, I realized, wasn't about having everything put together and complete. It's about being in a dynamic, ongoing process of constructing and deconstructing as you gain greater understanding about yourself and the world. My static concept of one day wearing the crown of maturity on Park Place Avenue was being taken back down to the studs.

Honestly, I rarely admire adults who play it safe, follow the rules, and stay in the same loveless marriage or job. I'm attracted to people who take risks, fail hard, get messy, and love fearlessly—the no-bullshitter types who are raw, vulnerable, and authentic. My former idea of security resembled the permanency of the lighthouse I lived by: an unwavering beacon of safety. But now I was drawn out into the depths of churning water. The waves, the wind, the unknown called my name out beyond where the light shone.

So, with my mom as my new purpose, I resigned from my job. Before doing so, I told my students what was happening—that my mom was dying, and I needed to be with my family in Oregon. They wholeheartedly supported my choice, but their faces conveyed the angst of abandonment.

"Ms. A., what about our letters to O Space?"

The letters were sacred totems of these kids' dreams. I wanted them to understand and never forget that they possessed an important voice in our community, that they mattered, that each of them mattered to me.

"Oh, I'm taking them to O Space, as promised, and I'll be sure to let you know what happens. Your letters are amazing. As are each one of you."

My eyes welled with tears. "I'm sorry I have to leave right when we were beginning to have fun. I'm really sorry, you guys."

As I left the building with wet cheeks, I shut the door of a 10-year teaching career. Though I felt relief knowing that I had done the right thing for myself and my family, I had no job now, no partner to help offset the bills, and two kids who were eager for Christmas presents and surprises. I was honestly scared stiff. Fortunately, the pressure of being Santa Claus forced me to act without overthinking it. I needed to make magic happen fast.

4. FLOWER PEDDLER OF VASHON

When life gives you lemons, you paint that shit gold.

- Album by Atmosphere

Once at home, I started frantically rummaging for quarters in the couch cushions. Searching for other swift solutions, I went down into the basement to find my old toolbox. As I rummaged through it, looking for anything to hold on to, I discovered two things: an empty aerosol can and a dusty photo of my kids when they were younger. Nothing inspired me more than the image of my babies looking to me as captain of their childhood. I was determined to show them that love wins, even when life throws you a sloppy mess. I picked up the rusty spray can and looked closely. I couldn't imagine why it was in my toolbox, but when I thought about it, a smile painted over my face of desperation.

When I was in my 20s, I dated an artist who crafted unique, funky metal flowers out of old aerosol cans. He also did graffiti, so he found empty cans littered all over hot spots where people painted. He sold a ton of these flowers at art shows and through galleries in Seattle and Portland. They cost next to nothing to construct—trash made into treasure—and were awesome yard art.

Finding that old can shifted the tide. I knew how to make these flowers, and with Christmas coming, I had the idea to make wreaths out of the spray cans by cutting them into stars and flowers. This was it. I even knew where I could get abandoned cans at a popular graffiti spot in Olympia. I jumped in the car and drove straight there with as many empty grocery sacks as I could carry. I parked along the railroad tracks and headed for the overpass where people did graffiti. I ran down the tracks, past a bustling homeless camp, to the unlikely spot. Hallelujah! It was a graveyard of cans. I felt like the luckiest kid at an Easter egg hunt. I walked back to my car laden with bags that rattled and clattered—musical garbage to my ears.

I set up a workshop in a friend's small shed in town and got to work. After so much had been ripped away from me, I felt like the Renaissance Woman of Vashon, crafting her way out of impending doom. I cut cans with tin snips until my palms were raw and the fumes from old paint spun me sideways. The weekend before Thanksgiving, I opened a humble storefront out the front door of the shed and started hustling my flowers to the quaint, crafty stores all over town. I quickly became known as the metal flower peddler of Vashon Island.

What happened next was nothing short of one of those holiday miracles that grace the classic movies we love. I was making more money—cash money—than I had ever made in one month. I went from having $50 to my name to having $500 a day from selling reworked garbage. I felt in charge, standing at the helm of my life. This much-needed gain turned the tides of my self-confidence as I could see that I had the power to steer my way through the storm and find creative ways to keep myself afloat as well as pay for my kids to have Christmas, which honestly guided and drove my tinkering passion.

The metal flower peddler of Vashon in her workshop, 2015.

5. THE BIG QUESTIONS

You carry all the ingredients to turn your life into a
nightmare – don't mix them! You have all the genius
to build a swing in your backyard for God. That sounds
like a hell of a lot more fun. Let's start laughing, drawing
blueprints, and gathering our talented friends.

- Hafiz

While crafting my way to immediate success with
my spray can flower business, I fell in love with working
with my hands. My favorite classes in high school had
been Wood Shop and 3-D Art. But I carried a near-per-
fect GPA throughout, so my advisors steered me toward
AP classes. I started attending college early through the
Running Start Program, burying my passion for tinkering
and constructing in a decade of acquiring college degrees.
Deep in my heart lay a smoldering desire to learn how
to build and even, one day, to build my own home.
I wanted someone to see and believe in the little girl inside
of me who didn't want to take notes and read books,

to acknowledge the *real* me who wanted to get dirty, run power equipment, and make cool shit.

My lifelong buddy Nate knew everything there was to know about the building process. In high school, Nate won the award for best attendance. He also rode a dirt bike onto the field during the Homecoming football game in his underpants, wearing a brown bag on his head, causing total mayhem. Nate is the type to work hard and play 10 times harder. Now in his mid-30s, Nate was a project manager for a huge construction firm in Seattle, making more money than all of my friends combined who had followed the college track.

With Thanksgiving approaching, I asked Nate to join me for a holiday beverage. We got together every now and then to catch up and share laughs. This time I had an agenda. I planned to ask him if I had a chance in hell of getting hired as a carpentry apprentice on the island as a middle-aged woman with zero experience.

I figured it would be wise to have a couple beers before diving into my true intentions for our conversation. Then I looked Nate in the eyes and said, "Buddy, I've got a real doozy for you."

He looked appropriately curious.

"So, I just quit my job teaching and I want to work in construction. Is there anyone you know who would consider teaching me how?"

Nate took a long drink, looking up to the ceiling, and set down his beer with a thud. Time crept by like a sloth as I held my breath. The bar seemed on pause as well.

"Well, you are totally fucking nuts, but we already knew that. There's only one guy who will consider hiring you without experience. His name is Don. He's a good guy. A bit of a ladies' man but not the gross kind. He actually likes to teach people and might need help on his crew right now."

I exhaled and took a sip. Bar activity resumed.

Hope. I had hope and hope had a name: Don, a semi-raucous island contractor. I was thrilled. I had a tangible person out there who might be able to ignite my inner builder. I threw the remainder of my warm, cheap beer back and gave Nate a heartfelt hug goodbye.

Fast-forward to mid-January 2016. I had done some research about Don, found his phone number, and started imagining my pitch to him. Cold-calling him sounded terrifying, but I needed work badly. The holiday-driven metal flower industry waned after Christmas. A new year, with new bills, awaited me.

It was a rainy afternoon, and my kids were with their dad. I decided to take myself out for a glass of wine at the Hardware Restaurant, one of the nicer spots to grab a bite on the island. As I walked up to the bar, greeting the familiar bartender, I realized Don was sitting right in front of me with an open seat next to him. Thanks to investigating Don on social media, I knew exactly what he looked like. There he sat with long amber hair, little round glasses, and a deep-seated smile in the creases of his cheeks.

What did I do? I plunked my ass right down next to him. We started talking about the weather. We realized his wife's kids were my age and that we had several mutual friends. Then I went for it. I grabbed my glass of wine, took a nervous gulp, and started rambling.

"Don, I have a big and unusual ask. It might seem like it's coming out of nowhere, but let me share a little story with you." I told him about my conversation with Nate. Don, of course, knew Nate well, being the local icon he was. I told him how I was in a big transition in my life, having left my teaching career, and that I wanted to learn construction.

"My dream is to build, Don. To learn how to build things and eventually to build my own house. But I have to tell you that I could be a terrible builder. I don't have any experience. Basically, I'm a 35-year-old woman who can't put IKEA furniture together, even when following the instructions."

He looked at me earnestly then nodded his head. "That's OK. This sounds fun. I love teaching people, especially women, my craft. They pay better attention than dudes do. So, when do you want to start, Julia?"

Remember how the bar seemed at a standstill when I was sitting with Nate waiting for his response? Well, in this moment, my heart flatlined. I was on full pause. *What? Wait. For real?*

"You want to hire me even though I've never built anything?" I whispered reluctantly, as though he might change his mind at any moment.

"Yep. How much do you want me to pay you? Twenty-five dollars an hour OK to start?"

At this point, I just started laughing uncontrollably. The combination of nerves, being dumbstruck, and actualizing the first step toward becoming a builder blew my fucking mind. We clinked glasses and looked each other in the eye. Something brilliant was being born from this leap into the unknown.

Don paused and said, "You're never going to regret this, Julia. Being a builder is the best gig in the world.

I can't wait to look back on this moment with you and remember how we started this journey together."

I knew he was right. That no matter where this choice took me, it would be a step toward manifesting a new life for myself and my kids. And that I had the heart of a builder even if I couldn't hammer a nail straight.

6. THE LAST HURRAH

The world is so exquisite, with so much love and moral depth, that there is no reason to deceive ourselves with pretty stories for which there's little good evidence. Far better, it seems to me, in our vulnerability, is to look Death in the eye and to be grateful every day for the brief but magnificent opportunity that life provides.

- Carl Sagan

With breakfast in their bellies, my children eagerly engaged my dad in a cutthroat game of Go Fish. They delighted in my parents coming for a visit from Oregon and had drafted a tight schedule of activities for Grandma and Grandpa. I was thrilled to tell them some good news, finally, that beyond making garbage into art, I had scored a real job in construction earning a decent wage right out of the blocks. They were delighted for me.

I was washing up the last of the dishes when my mom approached. She looked at me. She had a secret, I could tell.

"Let's get ready for our lunch date," she whispered. "What do you think?"

Perplexed by her offer, as we had just eaten, I flashed her a curious smile. We had a long-standing tradition of a noon rendezvous, just the two of us feasting and delving into a myriad of conversational topics. It was sacred mother-daughter time, so when she called me to court, I never questioned her intentions. I kissed the heads of those blissfully lost in play with Grandpa, and we headed to the car.

Once we were in, my mom grabbed my hand and looked me in the eyes. "This is the last time I will be able to come and visit you before my body craps out. Here's what I want to do, sweetie. Drive us to the grocery store. Buy me a bottle of white wine, yourself a bottle of red, and then we'll head to Dockton Park. I have things I need to tell you."

At that moment, I realized my mother was dying—not in some far-off future but soon. All the talk about cancer, treatments, lack thereof, and hospice had not prepared me for the sudden acknowledgment that I was losing my mother now. Like watching sand slipping through an hourglass, this was it. Our last hurrah.

"You got it, Momma." I wasn't drinking because I was emotionally at war with myself and alcohol fueled the enemy. But I was going to imbibe with my mother on this, our last lunch. So off we went, buying wine at 10 in the morning. No food. We didn't have time for that. We marched back to the car and drove straight to the park.

A bitter rain pelted the car. We parked in the upper parking lot looking out into the gray face of winter.

"Honey, I'm so sorry I'm leaving you right now when I know you really need me."

"Please don't feel bad, Mom. I'm gonna be OK. Things are turning around for me. I know I'm gonna be OK, I promise you."

She swallowed hard. Reaching around our bottles, she found my hand.

"Whatever happens with me, know that I love you. And that my love will always be with you."

"I know, Mom. Goddamn, this is so hard. I want to take you away from this, like we're Thelma and Louise."

"Just don't go over the cliff with me, OK?"

Raising our bottles, we drank. Soon the car was filled with our laughter, rich stories, reflections, and overflowing gratitude. Everything came flying out of our shared 35-year-old cornucopia of memories. As we neared the bottom of our bottles, my mother was preparing for a last toast. Pouring into her paper cup, she missed it completely, hosing the entire center console in sweet elixir. Tears of anguish and hilarity engulfed us whole.

Several hours had passed. It was time to take Mom home. Like bringing a drunk teenager in after curfew, I snuck her past the watchful eyes of my father and tucked her into bed. She definitely needed a nap. I lifted the blanket up to her cold hands and put my lips to her cheek, kissing her tears.

"Sleep well, Momma." Her eyes closed, and I stood there marveling at each breath she took.

A glimpse from my mom's final visit, the Last Hurrah.
Vicki and I, February 2016.

7. THE ART OF DECONSTRUCTION

You don't learn to walk by following rules. You learn by doing and falling over.

- Richard Branson

My first day working in construction was like my first day of kindergarten. I was fucking terrified. I put on my stiff new Carhartt overalls, loaded up my tool belt, and prayed that I wouldn't embarrass myself too badly. In my history of "adulting," I had never attempted to get paid for something that I had no idea how to do. Teaching, albeit a madhouse, was safe because I had followed a logical pathway of acquiring higher education to lead a group of kids as a so-called professional educator. I was great at loving kids and good enough at teaching them. But building was as foreign to me as jumping out of a plane. People did it, but I sure didn't.

Don was smart. He didn't start me off constructing. When I showed up to work, he took me straight into a putrid, 1970s green bathroom in a new client's house.

"This shitty bathroom is coming down to the studs, Julia. You ready?" Don handed me a crowbar with a sly smirk.

Studs. Hot guys or something inside of walls that you want to screw into when hanging heavy shelves and pictures. I looked at the crowbar in my hands, perplexed and anxious.

"What's the right way to do this, Don? I have no idea how to begin."

"Here's lesson one. Trust yourself. Do you trust yourself, Julia?"

No, no, I didn't trust myself in this moment. Not at all. But I knew Don wasn't asking me about my relationship to bathroom demo.

"I trust myself when I know what to expect but not when I don't know what's going to happen. Like, I don't know what's inside this wall. There must be electrical wires and maybe plumbing. I don't want to damage anything unknowingly."

Don looked at me, paused, and kicked his boot straight into the drywall, creating a ragged hole.

"You're right, Julia. There are things in the walls to be mindful of. But you will only find out if you start exploring. Take a risk and kick the wall."

He pointed to a place about a foot above the floor.

"Here? Are you sure?"

"Go!"

I took a deep breath and kicked the wall like I was sending a soccer ball down the field. The brittle drywall crumbled, and there, I discovered my first stud.

"Good. Now let me tell you about what's inside this wall before I have you take all the drywall off."

Don led me through a construction version of the "Dem Bones" song, outlining how the meat of the wall connected to the skeleton. It made so much sense that I quickly grew confident I could demo without destroying the internal framework. A bubbling trust emerged, and I beamed with pride to understand what was inside a wall.

"I can beat the shit out of this," I thought. "Yes, I can. I've got this." By day's end, on my first day of builder's school, I was covered like a gypsum miner in white powder, grinning from ear to ear.

"Now wait to see how we put all of this back together. You'll really be impressed." Don locked the client's house, and we left to grab a beer in town to celebrate work well done.

8. OPEN DOORS

The things you do for yourself are gone when you are gone, but the things you do for others remain as your legacy.

- Kalu Ndukwe Kalu

By early March 2016, I had broken in my overalls and solidified a way to keep my promise to my middle school class of visionaries. I couldn't teach full-time, but I could advocate and work to manifest their dreams at the art center called Open Space. After a round of heartfelt emailing, Amanda, the executive director of Open Space, wanted to create a part-time position for me to do teen outreach. This would allow me to also pursue my desire to learn how to build and still be able to spend time with my family.

"Girl, hustle over here and put this weenie in your mouth." Amanda opened the microwave door and grabbed the steaming hot frankfurter, tossing it onto my lunch plate. It was "Hot Dog Wednesday" at Open Space, and whether or not you liked nuked sausages, you were going to eat like you meant it.

We settled into a strategic planning meeting, trying not to get mustard on our pants, and revisited the teens' letters to Open Space.

"Dear Open Space, I'm home alone a lot and want a place to go after school that has cool people who I can talk to, and if I need homework help, they can be there for me."

"Dear Open Space, there's nothing to do here unless you have money. Vashon sucks. Can you make it suck less for us?"

Amanda looked at me with piercing conviction.

"We can do this," she said. "Not only can we do this, but we can figure out how to do it for free. These kids deserve so much better than they have been given by this privileged island."

Like the producer of a Broadway musical, Amanda always had coffee in hand. Within a few hours of working by her side, I learned to prepare it exactly how she liked it. "I'll take a little coffee with my cream, thank you." And she wasn't kidding. With a fashion sense straight from the streets of Milan, she walked the halls waving her goblet of caffeine, professing elaborate plans to make Open Space the next Carnegie Hall.

By the end of the week, we were brainstorming bosom buddies, and I had survived my first microwaved hot dog. Amanda immediately took me under her protective wing, like a fierce older sister who would set me straight about men, money, and makeup. I treasured the intuitive way she knew exactly what to say and do in any given situation. The last time I drove down to Oregon to visit my mom in hospice, Amanda was on the phone, coaching me through every painstaking mile back home.

Together with our passionate hearts, we were primed to take this island that totally sucked for teens and turn it into a place of connection and creativity. Amanda and I were hell-bent on making Open Space the official incubator of adolescent magic. And so, we read and reread those letters until we knew exactly where to begin.

Amanda and I (the mustachioed banana) running front of house for an Open Space fundraising event, 2016.

9. BUILDER BUDDY FOR LIFE

I would rather walk with a friend in the dark than alone in the light.

- Helen Keller

One afternoon, Don took me to a new job site, an upgrade of a rustic beach bungalow kitchen. I entered to discover an attractive guy standing in the kitchen whom I had recently taken notice of at an Open Space art show. He looked like Bruce Springsteen's twin brother. Yummy. I felt a pang in my chest. Maybe my heart hadn't died just yet.

"So, Don, this is the babe you hired with no experience." He shifted all his attention to me. "Howdy, I'm Craig." I flushed as he continued, "How are you liking it in construction so far?" He looked down at the dirt and dust on his arms and smirked up at me.

"So far, so good. I've still got all my fingers, and Don hasn't fired me yet."

"Good on you. It's nice to meet you. Julia, right? I think I saw you the other night at that show."

He had seen me too. Noted.

Like an ungrounded connection, sparks flew between us. He was older than me by quite a bit, but I could taste his magic and I wanted more. Don and I had driven separately, so when he left for another meeting, I quickly found a task to warrant my stay. I started loading the demo rubble into a garbage bag. When I looked up at Craig, he was looking right at me.

"So, what's your story?" Craig leaned against the skeletal remains of an old countertop.

"Oh Lord, it's a real whiz popper, Craig. I've been going through a series of unfortunate events."

I wasn't sure about being 100 percent transparent with how fucked up my life was, especially since I might have a chance to jump Bruce Springsteen's bones in the near future.

"Well then, why construction? You look a lot smarter than this kinda work." Craig banged against loose cabinetry with his hammer to accentuate his point. "I've been trying to quit this building shit for years."

His question surprised me. All I desired was the opportunity to learn how to build, so the idea of it being unworthy took me aback.

"This is my dream, Craig. Not to show up looking cute in a pair of Carhartt's, but to build a home for my family."

He nodded longingly and looked away.

"I'm going through some real shit too."

He took a long pause. "I'm getting divorced and being forced to sell my dream home. I pictured taking my last breath in that house. I've put so much into it over the years—pretty much all of me." He was still looking away from me, but I could sense the anguish on his face.

"A whole lotta my heart is in that home."

"Shit, I'm really sorry, Craig. That must be horrible. I'm going through some pretty fucked-up stuff too, if it's any consolation."

He looked at me as if to say, *Go for it.* The levy broke. I told him about leaving a decade of teaching. About divorcing Jake and being alone at the lighthouse. Of my mom's terminal cancer and how hard it was to be so far away from her.

We stood in that torn-up kitchen for two hours, sharing, listening, and holding space for each other's pain. Standing together in a busted-up cabin, we discovered an instant and profound bond between us. We were both deep in the mess of our lives, but now we were no longer alone.

I wanted to hold him against my chest, but when I checked my watch, it was time to leave. "I've got to get home. Jake's dropping my kids off at the lighthouse. Will I see you tomorrow?"

"Yep, I'll be back here bangin' on shit in the morning."

We both chuckled. I shut the door, eager to reopen it.

I overthought every aspect of the next morning. After sharing such an intimate exchange with Craig, I wasn't sure how to return to the nuts and bolts of construction with my crewmate. What I really wanted was to dive back into our conversation. Awkward and yearning, I showed up at the bungalow ready to learn how to tile a kitchen backsplash. Thank God Don was there. He had no idea how much interference he was running. I needed specific, hands-on instruction to begin tiling. Craig was busy knocking out a wall separating a master bathroom from the kitchen. We accomplished an amazing amount of work that day, all while laughing at each other's jokes and singing along to Tom Petty playing in the background.

Craig and Don had known each other a long time, and Craig joined forces with Don a handful of years ago. As a result, there was a familial vibe, like two brothers throwing levity at each other between the piercing hit of nail to board.

Suddenly, it was lunchtime, and we were all starving. I went over to my bag and pulled out a salad. When I turned around, there was Craig, down on both knees lowering his body to the floor. Was he bowing down to me? What the hell was happening?

"Julia," he said, lifting his head, "when Don said he hired a chick who couldn't build, I figured you might last a week. But you're doing one hell of a job tiling. And you're really fun to work with. Right, Don?" Don was around the corner and had been oblivious until Craig called him.

I looked at Craig humbly positioned below me and then to the kitchen wall I had freshly tiled.

"Well, shit, thanks. But you gotta get up now, Craig. I'm getting embarrassed."

"No, no, I actually can't because I have a bad knee." He hammed up his frozen state on the ground, and at this point, Don came over.

"Can I video this?" Don had already started videoing. "It's like you're the Mother Mary of Construction, Julia. You're blessing us goons with your grace. And Craig, how come you never get on your knees for me?"

Though normally quick with my tongue, I had no rebuttal. I was in shock and experiencing a trifecta of intrigue, honor, and humiliation.

"OK, seriously, get up, Craig. You're really starting to freak me out."

Craig rose with a hearty chuckle, and I turned to Don who had a shit-eating grin on his face. "I didn't know I was hiring 'a chosen one.' You just keep surprising me, Julia.

"Don't worry, Craig," Don continued, "I'll buy you some kneepads because my guess is that this won't be the last time Julia will floor you."

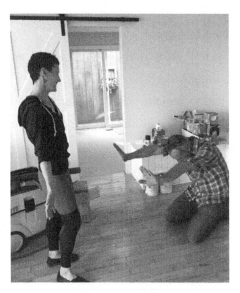

Craig and I at the beach bungalow in a moment
of spontaneous worship, 2016. Sorry, Craig.

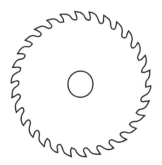

MOM AND SPRINGSTEEN

With a frosty Budweiser in hand, my mom lifted her lighter to the sky in solidarity with the 10,000 fans packed in the Tacoma Dome. Bruce Springsteen was belting out his 9/11 tribute "Into the Fire" to a crowd of bandana-wearing, cigarette-smoking, working-class heroes. The horrific events that swallowed the Twin Towers had occurred just a year prior, and the audience wore the recent trauma wet on their collective sleeves.

My mom's wish for her 52nd birthday was to see the Boss live in concert. I did what a devoted daughter does: manifest her mom's fantasy in the flesh. I bought the tickets online, spending more money than I ever had as a 22-year-old college kid accustomed to $5 covers at shows.

My mom shopped religiously at a bargain store on the island, so she had an extensive acrylic sweater collection that reflected her prudence. But when she got ready to see Bruce, I noted the extra time and care she took with herself. Applying blush to her cheeks as carefully as one would caress a newborn, she looked into the mirror with an arousing enjoyment of herself I had never witnessed. The elegant blouse she selected must have been hidden deep behind the cheap knockoffs. It was at this moment that I realized she was preparing for the hottest date of her life.

When we arrived at the Tacoma Dome, hundreds of people were gathered, decorated in the brightest shades of red, white, and blue, crooning classic Springsteen songs.

My mom lit a cigarette, grinning like the Cheshire cat. "Honey, this is a dream come true. We haven't even stepped inside, but I feel completely overjoyed."

I had never seen my mom look so alive. So feminine and free. So damn rock 'n' roll.

"I'm so excited to experience this with you, Mom. You deserve to have your heart on fire like this."

She started singing his song "I'm on Fire" as the crowd starting filing in. My mom stubbed out her cig, and we jumped into the river of America.

I didn't understand my parents' relationship. They rarely hugged and never kissed. It seemed like they were more like business partners than wife and husband. I certainly had never seen my mom like this—embodied, sexy, passionate, expectant.

I bought us both beers, and we found a spot on the floor.

"I've got to get closer. I want to really see him," she said. "To be with him."

The crowd was as dense as a thunder cloud, but she wound her way toward the stage as though she had done it a hundred times. I watched her go, knowing she had waited for this moment her whole life. My play-it-safe Virgo mother was headed to the mosh pit.

Through the sea of heads, her wild hair and unusual height lifted her up like the crest of a perfect wave.

When the lights went dark, hollering screams brought the returning spotlight directly on the Boss. He looked like the god of Levi 501s. My eyes darted back to my mom. Every part of her was in revelry. She was screaming. Shaking. Waving. Crying.

In this year following the tragic events of 9/11, the room was healed by his very presence. People holding hands. Arms wrapped around strangers. Red plastic cups cheering in the name of America's Revival.

My mom danced the entire set like a teenager liberated from a parent's watchful eye. When we met up after the encore, she appeared untethered, sweaty, and so fucking happy. She lit a cig outside of the venue and blew out a cloud of smoke while talking.

"You know, I'd leave your father in a heartbeat if Bruce asked me to join him on tour."

Not only did I know this to be true, but I also felt it powerfully in my own soul. I wanted to know more about this wild woman who lived inside my mom. I thought about running back inside to try to find Bruce. Instead, we walked to the car, bobbing our heads to the melodies that played on.

10. THE GOOD, THE BAD, AND THE SHIT

Most people are afraid of suffering. But suffering is a kind of mud to help the lotus flower of happiness grow. There can be no lotus flower without the mud.

- Thich Nhat Hanh

"Mama, why do bad things happen to good people?" Mirabelle looked up at me after kicking a rock into the ditch. Her delicate hands were playing with the dangling straps of her backpack.

"Can you give me an example of what you're thinking about?" The school bus was coming, and I hoped to unpack the crux of her inquiry before sending her off into her day.

"Why is Grandma dying even though she is a wonderful Grandma? Why will I never see her again even though I love her and want her to be with me forever?"

I envisioned my mom as I had last seen her in Oregon, lying in her hospital bed hooked up to morphine, breathing heavily as though her chest was filling with cement. My eyes flooded with the depth of Mirabelle's question.

"Grandma loves you very much, honey. She doesn't want to be leaving you or me or any of us. But sometimes things happen that we can't control and that don't make sense. And we have to accept the bad and go on living our lives."

That wasn't the answer I wanted to give, but it was true. I spotted the school bus at the top of the hill rumbling toward us.

"I guess there is some bad out there because it helps us know the good. Right, Mom?"

The brakes squealed, and the bus came to a halt in front of us.

"Yes, you're right. Let's keep talking about this, OK?"

Mirabelle nodded and jumped up the bus steps. The driver smiled and off they went.

As I walked back to the lighthouse, Mirabelle's question consumed me. Here I was experiencing profound loss, yet in the midst of it, I had begun living my dream of learning to build with Don and had taken action to manifest the dreams of a deserving group of teens at Open Space. Like a set of scales, I could see the shit in one hand and the gold in the other. If it hadn't been for going through a separation from Jake and losing my mom to cancer, I never would have met Don or Amanda.

My throat constricted as if I were choking down a glass of cold mud.

I pictured myself at the garbage dump as a child, back in the '80s when they made giant piles of trash on a piece of cheap land. Once a month, my dad would take me in our old Ford truck to drop off our trash, and I absolutely loved it. The rotten fragrance of disregarded living could not obscure the magic of broken things. Looking beyond the waste, I saw a mecca of mankind. I remember spotting a broken toy doll and thinking that it was the most beautiful creation. When I went to touch it, my dad reprimanded me.

"That's trash, Julia. We've got to leave it here because it's nasty."

But I knew better. Just as Mirabelle had mentioned at the bus stop, without the bad, how would we ever know the good? And sometimes, the two blurred as one. There was glory in our garbage if we looked beyond what we could simply see. Our messes weren't always working against us. In fact, they contained fragments of our greatest beauty and potential.

11. MOURNING TIDE

The sea is emotion incarnate. It loves, hates, and weeps. It defies all attempts to capture it with words and rejects all shackles. No matter what you say about it, there is always that which you can't.

- Christopher Paolini

Staring out at a seaweed mosaic, I pictured my mom leaving her body. Weeks had passed with her in a state of unconsciousness, yet she hung on, adrift, a ghost ship with sails filled by an uncertain wind.

"Please, please, Mom, let go," I uttered over and over standing in my kitchen. "No more pain. No more suffering."

Then the call came. It was my dad. It was 3:30 p.m., April 24, 2016.

"She's gone, Julia. It's over."

The tide was coming in, rushing over the broken shells and kelp beds. The sand disappeared beneath the water's tendrils.

"What happens next, Dad?"

He didn't answer the question. Perhaps he couldn't. Or maybe he didn't hear me through the static of loss.

Mirabelle and Dockton were playing in their room nearby. I wasn't sure how to proceed with death now sitting on my shoulder. I didn't want to scare them. I didn't want to hide the truth from them. When they saw my face appear in the doorway to their bedroom, they froze.

"Did she die, Mom? Is Grandma dead?" Mirabelle stood up.

"Yes, Grandma left her body and is free. She's not hurting anymore." I choked on the clot of emotions that filled my throat then wrapped my arms around them both.

Dockton pulled back. "But where did she go, Mama?" Being his beautiful 3-year-old self, he began looking around as though she might be hidden somewhere in the room.

"She's in her spirit body, Doc. Now she can go anywhere, and I bet she is right here to give you hugs. She loves you both so much."

When I awoke the next morning, I threw on my overalls and hurried out the door to get my kids to school and daycare. I watched Doc still looking for my mom around corners.

Once I was alone, I succumbed to the piercing agony of grief. I needed to scream, and I did. I banged my hands against the steering wheel. Fuck. Anger wasn't going to help, but I had to allow it. And I needed to show up to work and be functional enough to use power tools. I gave myself 15 minutes to erupt and then another five to put myself back together so I could get my ass to the job site.

When I showed up, Don looked at me with the same fixed stare as my kids.

"Julia, what's up?"

"It's my mom. She's gone. She passed away yesterday afternoon. And I don't really know how to do this right now."

"You don't have to know how to do anything. Let's get you out of here."

Don put his hand on my shoulder and directed me toward his truck. I felt my mother's spirit sweeping around me like a wind of protective assurance.

"Come on," he said as we walked toward his truck. "Let's go out for breakfast. If you want to talk, that's great. And if you don't, that's OK too." As Don rolled toward town, I nodded, looking out the window. Being seen like this was hard. But I couldn't hide any part of myself, inside or out. I was awash with grief.

We walked back into the restaurant where I had first met Don. When the server approached us, I explained that I was a hot mess because my mom had just died. She swiftly brought me a fresh donut and a hot cup of coffee.

"Thank you so much, Don. I was going to try and work today because I didn't want to let you down. But it is really comforting to be here with you, surrounded by such kindness."

"I remember your mom, Julia. She was such a beautiful woman. And so are you. She's really proud of you, you know."

Don held my hand and smiled. In this moment, I felt her close by. I could smell the floral musk that wafted from her hair. Was that her smoking a cigarette outside the window, grinning at us with her thin lips?

Near the end of breakfast, Don offered to buy me a drink for a toast to my mom. Tequila was her favorite liquor, so we ordered two shots.

"Here's to your mom and her legacy of love. Thank you, Momma." Don and I met eyes, connected glasses, and threw back the warm elixir. We were two combatants of life, and a heartfelt comradery was being born out of the depths of what makes us most viscerally human: love and death.

Don and I, 2016.

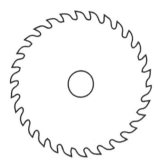

MOM'S ASHES

he unscrews the lid.
i peer into
the depths of a jar.

we hiked up the bluff
of my childhood haunt
to help fly her home.

mom's ashes clutched
in dad's palm,
a bottle of wine
in mine.

we take turns talking
about her,

tears choking
syllables
from our sentences.

a breathless pause,
we watch her rise,
a tempestuous wind
engulfing us whole.

i look to dad,
ash matted to face,
sobbing, smiling,
both of us standing cliffside,
coated in mom.

raising a dusty bottle,
we drank to her love,
her love into us,
sipping stardust.

12. THE DREAM TEAM

Until one is committed, there is hesitancy, the chance to
draw back, always ineffectiveness. Concerning all acts of
initiative (and creation), there is one elementary truth, the
ignorance of which kills countless ideas and splendid plans:
that the moment one definitely commits oneself, then
Providence moves too. All sorts of things occur to help one
that would never otherwise have occurred. A whole stream
of events issues from the decision, raising in one's favor all
manner of unforeseen incidents and meetings and material
assistance, which no man could have dreamt would have
come his way. I have learned a deep respect for one of
Goethe's couplets: Whatever you can do, or dream you
can, begin it. Boldness has genius, power, and magic in it!

- William Hutchison Murray

"Look, I'm either joining the Peace Corps and moving
to Africa or coming to the island to be closer to you and
the kids."

My dad was leveled by the loss of my mom. And
though I could see him in a Jeep exploring the Great
Savannah, I didn't want him out in the world with a
broken heart. I knew his very survival depended on his
love for us and us loving him through this pain, so I told
him that the Peace Corps could wait. My dad quickly

sold their house in Oregon and was on the island within a week of my mom's death.

Don invited my dad to camp out on his 50-foot sailboat down in Quartermaster Harbor. As a former sailor, I hoped boat life would comfort him. He seemed to take to it, deciding to buy his own boat and become a live-aboard down at the marina.

On an idyllic evening, when my kids were both with Jake, I went down to share dinner and a bottle of wine with my dad. The water sparkled with evening warmth, and a gentle breeze kissed my cheeks. We were sitting across from each other, toe to toe, on the deck of his sailboat.

"So, I've got a question for you," he said, pausing for a sip of wine. "What are you doing with your life, Julia?"

I inhaled a mouthful of wine and looked out across the sea of boats docked around me.

"Well, I know I want to stay here on the island until the kids are done with school. And that I've fallen in love with construction. I want to keep building."

My dad smiled and reached his hand out to meet mine.

"I've got an idea, kid. Are you ready?"

I nodded with intrigue.

"I've been looking at properties for sale and found a really sweet one. What if we build a house together— you and Don build it; I design it and get the property?"

Holy shit. It took a lot to surprise me these days, but I hadn't seen this one coming.

"But the real question is, do you want to live with a cranky old man?"

We laughed and hugged and laughed and hugged some more. Yes, I was going to build my dream home with my unlikely new life partner: my dad. Yes, I wanted this even though I had no idea what I was signing up for. Yes, yes, YES!

Seventy-two hours after my dad and I had toasted to building a new life together, the winds of fate filled our sails. He put an offer down on the property, and we were off. I knew something was guiding this propulsion forward. My mother's spirit, definitely. Magic conjured by my dad's inspired action, most certainly.

"I know your mom is behind a lot of this." He teared up in the truth that we both held dear. "And I found an amazing woman who is the realtor that helped me find the property."

The existence of fairies in the forests of Vashon has been widely embraced and celebrated, mostly by those under age 10. Then there were the older believers. My dad had attracted one such sprite into his real estate dealings. Her name was Jean, and she happened to be Don's boat neighbor as well. (On Vashon, there are only two degrees of separation between most people.)

I first met Jean when I started working with Don, since real estate and construction are kissing cousins in local business. Her voice was like a fresh molasses cookie, deep and slow, and words fell sweetly off her tongue.

My dad had stumbled upon her while looking at properties online. They connected instantly. She knew of my mom's recent death and held my dad protectively in her grace. Jean crafted an irresistible offer, knowing that another potential buyer was hot on the property as well. Within 10 days of our commitment to buy and build on the island, the property was in our possession. The dream team of my mom, Jean, and my dad had knocked it out of the park and landed us in the wooded wonderland that I would soon call home.

It was time to get rolling. The first step with the construction site was to submit for a permit to build. In King County (Seattle being included within that boundary), acquiring a building permit is similar to gestation of an elephant. If you're lucky, you're talking a year out, and if you're unlucky, it could take as long as three. There was both need and desire to break ground and get construction underway. My position as caretaker at the lighthouse was temporary, and finding rental housing for my kids and myself was close to impossible. Add to that, my dad was lonely and uncomfortable down on his small sailboat that held few amenities.

Don's 35 years of permitting experience definitely was a game changer. Matched with my dad's career of architectural experience, their skills merged nicely in getting final plans developed quickly. I went with Don to submit the plans. When we walked into the permit office, it was clear he was famous.

"Don! You're back. How's it going?"

"Sarah, hello! Great. Got a really exciting new build we're about to start for this young lady and her family."

"Awesome. Congrats. Well, let's get this party started!"

This didn't mirror the hellish stories I had heard of the permitting experience. Don obviously was the permit whisperer. Or permit persuader.

As we walked out with the plan in motion for acquiring our permit, it hit me that my dream house would be born after all. And I would be the proud mama of this beautiful creation.

As we left, Don threw me an elbow. "I'm pretty good at this shit, right?"

Within a few weeks of submitting the permit, we cleared the buildable portion of the property, which was heavily wooded with third- or fourth-growth forest. My son brought his toy excavator and happily worked the land. My daughter would look around and ask me, "So, when's the house gonna show up?"

One day in late August, Don showed up to work with tears in his eyes.

"Julia, I've got some really bad news. Jean's got cancer, and it's terminal."

Jean had been diagnosed with a rare form of brain cancer. It was an aggressive form, and she had been told she would only have a few months left. How could such a beautiful light force be dying? Not again. It was unfathomable.

The last time I saw her was September 29 at a café on the island. Her golden spirit beamed. In the grip of her hug, I knew I would not see her again.

"I am forever grateful for what you did for my family, Jean. I love you so much."

"Julia, it was a true pleasure to help make your dreams come true. I can't wait to see the house you build with Don."

Jean passed away January 2017 on her boat that she loved. Though she never got to see my house completed, I imagine her and my mom coming by for a visit.

Don, Mirabelle, Susy (Don's wife), Dockton, Scott (my dad), and Craig the day the property was first cleared, 2016.

13. ECONOMY OF MOTION

Only someone who is ready for everything, who doesn't exclude any experience, even the most incomprehensible, will live the relationship with another person as something alive and will himself sound the depths of his own being.

- Rainer Maria Rilke

For many of us, one of our earliest memories of visceral pain is brutally crashing on a bike while learning how to ride. Oh, how freaking bad it feels to have major portions of our flesh connect with asphalt. But to achieve the freedom of flying down a hill on two wheels, there's simply no way of avoiding the fall. From car accidents to serious illnesses, surviving from bodily injury can require a few weeks of healing to many years of intensive rehabilitation. Some things we can never regain or rebuild. But one common attribute of survival, regardless of the outcome, is the ability to learn from and work through the hurt.

Small humans are gluttons for punishment. And they are so clever. I've always smiled at the idea of "childproofing" because inevitably kids go for the one danger they haven't experienced and adults have over-looked. Don't get me wrong; I don't want kids to electro-cute themselves because covering the outlets would limit their experiential learning. I'm talking about the illusion that we can keep pain out of the process of acquiring knowledge of ourselves and our power. Pain is required for deep, meaningful learning. Watching little kids do a face-plant when learning to walk, cry a bit because it hurts, then get right back up and try again is a raw lesson in resiliency.

Working in construction tests the human form daily. It teaches me that our bodies are both breakable and keen at recovering. From balancing on ladders to lifting heavy boards into place, not to mention those nasty splinters that bring the biggest guy on the crew to his knees, builders are faced with multiple challenges. Being a 110-pound woman amid this reality creates opportunities, as well as constrictions, within the learning process. I quickly ascer-tained how to make myself an asset rather than a liability. I learned that work involving attention to detail, like tiling, was my contribution, and that when it was time to lift a 400-pound beam into place, I'd take a step back from the action.

I paid close attention to how tools were used as well. I'd always heard, "The right tool for the right job," but honestly had never owned many tools other than art supplies. As I learned which tools were a necessity and how to use them, Don generously shared the most valuable tool—his philosophy about the Economy of Motion.

The Economy of Motion is simple yet hugely profound. Reduce wasted energy and time by planning out your steps in any process. Tool belts are fabulous support in being more efficient, especially when working up on a ladder. I realized that this principle could revolutionize my life. When getting my kids ready for school, making dinner, or packing for vacation, having a clear vision and mapped-out plan significantly improved the outcome. It reduced stress, both physical and emotional, and increased joy in whatever task needed to be accomplished.

My excitement grew as I began filling my toolbox with actual tools plus the gems Don was gifting me. Screwdriver. Measuring tape. Pencil. Trust—for myself and others. Collaborative skills. Consistent joy. I started seeing how building things was synonymous with building self, how the mess innate in building could be applied to life. Chaos was calmed by having a solid plan and holding the big picture in hand. Organization and planning allowed mundane work to have meaning.

I finally saw that the pain I had endured in losing my mom, my husband, and my career was propelling me to be the best learner I could be. To try harder. To ask more questions. To risk looking like an idiot for the sake of building my dream. Had I not known the hardship, I never would have left the comfort of what I had known for the unknown adventure. I could almost be grateful for what had felt like a curse. Like that 2-year-old sprawled on the ground after falling, I could look up and see myself living the life I had always wanted, running with greater confidence and clarity. That's what I was going to need in order to build my house—a whole lot of chutzpah. And a bunch of Band-Aids.

14. THE FOUNDATION

If you have built castles in the air, your work need not
be lost; that is where they should be. Now put the
foundations under them.

- Henry David Thoreau

It was *pour* day, which meant a whole load of concrete
was about to cement my dream into a hard-as-rock
reality. After spending the summer clearing and grading
our property, the first step was laying a strong foundation.
To some, the formation of a 30-foot by 30-foot slab of
concrete would appear insignificant. But to me, it person-
ified a solidity I had never felt. I was building my home
and, at the same time, developing a deeper trust of myself
and of the world.

"Julia, once the concrete sets, we can start framing.
Then everything will really begin to flow. You wait."

Don, Craig, and I watched the concrete cascade from
the pump hose as the workers performed a well-choreographed dance raking the slop smooth. I imagined my
kids chasing each other through the living room and my
friends sitting at my kitchen table sharing a meal with me,

all atop this solid mass. Once the concrete crew and truck left, I stood there in awe of my new foundation.

We all went for a beer to process this moment of fundamental, essential progress.

"Julia, can you fucking believe that you're really building your own house?" Craig brought his beer up to his dirty shoulder, inspiring a round of celebratory cheers. "To Julia, and her witchy ways of making magic happen."

No, no, I couldn't believe it. A few months prior to this moment, I couldn't build shit, I didn't have a dime and no property to my name. But now I was working with a team of amazing people to manifest my lifelong dream of building my own home.

It was on this early October day, sharing beers and having a glass of delicious wine with my new best friends, that everything started coming together in spite of what I didn't have when it all started. It was as if that conversation with Nate at the bar last Thanksgiving had conjured a council of magicians, spirit guides, and comedians to dramatically change my fate for the better, and I've learned that, even with losses and heartbreaks, the good guys really do win. At least for now. And no matter what, I had my foundation built. No one could take that away from me.

Craig, Don, and I standing on the
freshly poured foundation, fall 2016.

15. THE ASSAULT

It cannot be seen, cannot be felt, cannot be heard,
cannot be smelt. It lies behind stars and under hills,
and empty holes it fills. It comes first and follows after,
ends life, kills laughter.

- J.R.R. Tolkien

I was just coming off a monthlong high of building my house. I figured it was time to treat myself to a night out. It was the Saturday before Halloween, and the town bustled with ghouls and goblins. I went for a celebratory glass of wine at a local bar where I was a familiar face among many before attending a spooky play called *Darkness Illuminated*.

I left a generous tip for the bartender and drove to the art center, eager to experience live theatre and see Craig perform on stage. Acting was Craig's true passion, and I couldn't wait to witness him play the bad guy in the production. The venue was full of locals, and I mingled happily with old friends upon entering the lobby.

After about 10 minutes of chatting before curtain call, I realized something was profoundly wrong with me. I could hear and see everything happening, but my responses sat like rocks in my head. It was as though I was operating from outside of my body. I couldn't formulate sentences in response to what people were saying. What the fuck was happening? My brain's control panel was acting like a wire had been severed. And I felt horribly embarrassed and afraid.

The lights flashed, calling the crowd to their seats, and I found one near the aisle, hoping to recover and reengage in my special night out. After a few more minutes passed, my hearing was gone. I could see everything happening on the stage, but I was completely shut off from the audible world. I trembled in terror, convinced I was having a complete meltdown, or maybe it was the onset of a stroke. Sweat ran down my forehead. I had to escape. I ran to the door of the art center and stepped out into the parking lot, a sea of darkness spotted with colorful blobs of rain-soaked cars.

Where had I parked? I had arrived less than an hour ago, and it was as though I had never driven in my life. God dammit. I was out in the dark, in a familiar parking lot, lost. How could I be this fucked up after one glass of wine? After what must have been 25 minutes of hopeless searching, I stumbled upon my car. My pants were soaked up above my thighs as though I had been crawling over the rain-soaked ground. I fell into the driver's seat like a worn rag doll.

"Fuck! No! Why?" I yelled. I hated being out of control and felt like I was in a flash flood inside and out. As I sat in the driver's seat of my car, I noticed the faces of glowing jack-o'-lanterns set on the rail of a nearby business. It was as though they were mocking my unexplainable absurdity. The car dashboard showed it was 7:08 p.m. I blinked.

Then the long, horrible darkness consumed me.

The next morning, nothing made sense. I was returned to my car by the total stranger I had woken up next to, naked and in horrendous pain.

I got in and saw my phone. It had been left there in the center console. I would never leave my phone. When I looked at it, I realized I'd lost an entire night. So many missed calls lit the home screen. I sat, rocking myself, weeping in my car, shivering, trembling, just before dawn. I was alone with the darkness.

My dad. My kids. My friend. They thought I was dead. I fucking disappeared. Their messages told me they were out searching all night in the darkness for me, for any evidence of me, talking to anyone they could find, trying to follow clues.

I had done the unthinkable. I left and didn't come home. But I was alive. In my car. Broken but breathing.

I called my dad. He took me immediately to the ER. He knew something terrible had happened to me and demanded we get answers. A seizure maybe? I writhed in agony, battling flashbacks of waking up in bed next to the stranger. The nurse took my blood. Rape kit. I saw the bruises on my body. Rape kit. She saw them too. I shivered. I still couldn't see straight and had vertigo. I needed to vomit, but I sat there frozen.

"I've got the test results. You were drugged, Julia," the nurse standing over me stated.

"Drugged? How? What does that mean?" I asked.

"Have you heard of date-rape drugs? You have one in your system."

Drugged. I'd had one glass of wine at 5:30 p.m. in my hometown bar.

"The darkness," she explained, "is what happens when the drugs take effect. You will probably never remember the details about what happened. Maybe that's a good thing."

A good thing. Someone had released a serpent into my bloodstream. I had been consumed whole, turned inside out. I was grateful as hell to be alive, but I knew as I put my soiled clothes back on that I was deeply damaged. No part of me was like it had been the day before. Julia Harriet was still missing even though she had been returned to her family.

16. THE MONDAY AFTER

"God says we need to love our enemies. It hard to do. But it can start by telling the truth. No one had ever asked me what it felt like to be me. Once I told the truth about that, I felt free."

- Aibileen in **The Help,** *by Kathryn Stockett*

It's surprising how well the body can operate on automatic pilot after experiencing trauma. When I woke up the second morning after my assault, I entered my usual sunrise ritual in the hopes of avoiding the harsh reality that loomed over and inside of me. I opened the gate to the lighthouse, made my coffee with cream, read a few quotes while sitting in bed next to an open window, then headed to the shower.

As soon as I saw my naked body in the bathroom mirror, the facade of normalcy crumbled. Covered in bruises and scratches, I saw shame smeared all over my body. I was defiled and damaged. No amount of soap could wash away the brutal truth. I would never be the

Julia that I had been 48 hours ago. She died and woke up the victim of a violent assault.

That's when my survival systems kicked back in again. I left the bathroom and threw clothes on to get ready for work. I avoided looking at myself. I drove in silence to Open Space for a planning meeting about an upcoming fundraising event. Any sound—a song or a voice—would have fractured my false, fragile composure. At one point, the car veered slightly off the road, tires hitting the uneven gravel. I had forgotten I was even driving.

When I got to the parking lot at Open Space, my hands were trembling hard against the steering wheel and my legs were weak. I was barely able to park the car straight.

A moment later, Amanda came roaring up in her old Mercedes convertible, wearing her usual "gonna take Monday by the pants" smile.

I looked out my car window at her, watching her expression drop into pale concern. I slowly opened the door, but before I spilled out, she was there to catch me.

"Oh God, honey, what happened?"

Everything I'd been holding inside started to spill out like a ruptured dam. Nothing could hold back the anguish. I buried my head into her chest. I couldn't find the words. I couldn't even speak. She just waited, holding onto me.

"Something fucking horrible happened to me. I don't even know. But I got hurt really bad, Amanda."

She swept me into her car and wrapped me in a blanket from the back seat. Amanda was a Virgo, like my mom, and Virgos are masters of managing madness. I told her the few memories I had from my night of terror and the pieces from the next morning that I could remember, including what I had learned at the ER.

"I'm going to fucking kill this guy, Julia," she said. "Before I kill this guy, whoever he is, we're going to DOVE. It's a place with people who are trained to help people who have been hurt like you. They will know what to do." Then she wrapped me in loving assurance and roared out of the parking lot.

Disturbing thoughts ran laps in my head, recalling news of women who came out with their stories of being drugged and sexually assaulted and were blamed for their rapes; that simply by being in a bar alone, a woman was asking for it; that this would never happen to a good woman or a good mom, only to a whore.

I'd heard of DOVE. I thought it was an agency that served victims of domestic violence. I wasn't certain how that applied to me, but I didn't resist or question. In less than five minutes, we were at the office door, ringing a bell to be let in.

"Do you want me to come with you?"

"Yes. I can barely walk, I'm so scared, Amanda." I didn't know what to expect, but I knew I needed all the help I could get.

As we entered their office, an advocate greeted us warmly. Her name was Nyn, and she gestured for me to sit on a couch. As I sat, I felt the enormous weight of all I had been holding in and prayed silently for release. So far, sharing any part of my story caused it to become more real and more burdensome. Amanda held my hand. Words and tears poured out of me like a fire hose, and I felt trapped, as though I were on the third story of a building engulfed in flames. I didn't want to admit I was a victim or that I was now a broken person.

Nyn sat calmly with my anguish. She didn't tell me everything would be OK. Rather, she created a safe space for me to be seen, heard, and acknowledged.

"I believe you, Julia," Nyn said slowly, lingering on each word. "You didn't deserve any of what happened. It's not your fault, and we are going to help you heal because that's what we do." She looked into my eyes, past the torrent of suffering, straight into my core.

"Thank you. Thank you so much. Thank you." I kept saying thank you. I'm not sure how many times. Then Amanda interjected, "Can you also help those of us who love the hell out of Julia, so we don't go out and kill this fucker who hurt her?" Amanda always knew just what to say. I laughed for the first time in 48 hours.

At this point, Amanda took command of the conversation. Someone had to. I was still lost in the moment when Nyn had said, "I believe you." While Amanda talked about lawyers, counselors, acupuncturists, and advocates, I was visualizing a helicopter swooping down to pick me up out of a tumultuous sea. That was the moment when I felt there was hope, that I would come out of this darkness a survivor. That this wickedness wasn't mine and that I wasn't responsible. I didn't deserve it. Yes, I was someone's victim, but I wasn't going to let the villain win by freezing my heart. I would rebuild and rise. And I knew I would need to call forth a crew of family, friends, and healers to help me put myself back together again.

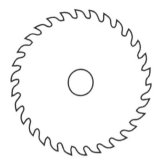

SNOW WHITE

Mud dripping off his chin, Keith kneeled in one of the larger puddles on the playground. Greg had tossed him in there, which, sadly, was a common playground occurrence. Often, Greg would come to school with bruises on his arms and face, once even around his neck. It appeared that Greg was being shown the ropes by a much bigger bully at home.

I witnessed the harassment from my place on the monkey bars. I could see Keith was crying, so I ran over to him. He was small for fourth grade and smelled like old carpet and pee. I didn't want to attract Greg's attention because a few months' prior, he casually punched me in the stomach for wearing an Oregon Ducks T-shirt to school. He was a Husky fan. But I had to do something.

"Keith, are you OK?"

I was extremely shy as a fourth grader and rarely talked to kids outside of my friend group. But I was worried he was hurt. No one else was doing anything.

"No, my mom is going kill me. He broke my glasses."

He was still in the puddle crying louder than before. I looked through the crowd of bustling kids for the playground aide but no luck.

"I bet your teacher can help. Let's go find her," I offered, helping him up. Mostly, I was worried that Greg would come back, and I'd end up sprawled out next to Keith in the mud.

Just as Keith was pulling himself upright, I felt a king crab grasp on my shoulder. Greg was behind me. I was at his total mercy.

"How sweet," he cackled. "Snow White likes Pee Wee."

My nickname was Snow White because I was the spitting image of her. And I was generally an adorable kid. When asked, "What do you want to be when you grow up?" for a class assignment, I responded quickly, "A nice person." I wanted people to like me.

But here I was, in the clutches of the school's cruelest playground villain. Keith was obviously no help, and my friends weren't the type to get involved.

I shut my eyes and took a deep breath. My dad had taught me some self-defense moves. Recently we practiced the drop, hit, run technique. I knew it was all I had. I dropped down to the ground like an anvil, which forced him to release my shoulder.

"What the hell?!" Greg said with surprise.

I couldn't figure out how to kick or hit him since he had been behind me and my dad had only practiced this skill with me once. But I rolled and it created enough space for me to get up and run for my life. Greg must have been shocked because he didn't follow me.

The bell rang. I took a deep breath. Like a fighter in the ring, I had escaped a major blow. This round.

17. TRUMPED

Anything that's human is mentionable, and anything that is mentionable can be more manageable. When we can talk about our feelings, they become less overwhelming, less upsetting, and less scary. The people we trust with that important talk can help us know that we are not alone.

– Fred Rogers

Eleven days after I was drugged and raped, Trump became the 45th President of the United States. Craig and I were in a bar in downtown Seattle witnessing the election results with a cohort of avid Democrats. At first, the space was alive with laughter, politically charged excitement, and connective energy. Quickly, however, the mood tanked, and the group began gasping, pained by the numbers rolling in. What was happening? Could the creep be creeping into office?

As a very recent victim of sexual violence, looking at Trump's pumpkin-faced pride on the big screen sickened me. Our weeping faces washed the collective hope from the room. Bad guys who do bad things can become leaders of the free world. Fuck this news. I'm out.

Craig and I abandoned our drinks and walked out into a city silenced in anguish.

"Julia, this is the worst day of my life," Craig announced, his arm slung over my shoulder as we paused before crossing the street to my car. "I can't believe it. I can't fucking believe he won. I don't want to be a man right now. Men are so fucked up."

"I know, Craig. I have spent my whole life believing in the power of good, and now it's just gone. I've got nothing."

We held each other, sobbing on the dimly lit street. Good had gone missing that night. Except we had each other.

The next day, Don, Craig, and I converged at my property to raise the first wall of my home. We exited our vehicles, into the pissing November rain, and approached one another like points of a triangle folding inward. Our six arms enveloped one another's sadness.

"You guys," I said, "I'm so broken right now." Don and Craig held me tighter, as though I was literally in shards.

Don suddenly perked his head up. "The only thing we can do is to build our way out of this pain. We have to make this better together."

"We love you, Julia. Let's put so much fucking love into these walls today that nothing can bring them down." Craig, crying, turned to grab his nail gun.

Don walked over to the lumber load and grabbed a 2x6. I nodded, looking down into my wet gloves. The only thing I could do was to start doing.

Without words, we lifted the first wall quickly into place and secured it to the base plate. That single exertion put a small piece of good back into place.

"Shit, I needed that. I don't know what I'd do without you two in these times."

Craig lit a cigarette, and we stood marveling at the first inkling of my house rising. "Let's get another one up fast."

As we erected more walls, our spirits followed in suit. After a day's work, we had all the exterior walls of the first floor constructed.

"Let me take your picture, Julia. Next to one of these walls." Don gestured where he wanted me, and I approached, wrapping my arms around the board. I held on for dear life because there was love to be found here, and we were acting as each other's scaffolding, lifting each other as we went.

Holding on to the frame postelection, 2016.

18. HILARY THE HEALER

You must let the pain visit.
You must allow it to teach you.
You must not allow it to overstay.

– Ijeoma Umebinyuo

"If you take Sitting Bull, Buddha, and Maya Angelou and put them all into one human, then you have Hilary," Betsey, the executive director of DOVE, stated as she took a sip of coffee with a little smirk of genius on her face. Her description of Hilary, the resident therapist at DOVE, had exceeded her own expectations. And I was certainly intrigued.

Betsey's daughter was in the same class as Mirabelle, so I would run into her while we waited to grab our kids from school. While standing in the hall, I learned a lot about her: she founded and directed an island nonprofit serving victims of domestic violence; she liked red wine and rambunctious costume parties; her husband was a personal pilot for famous people. She had a natural tenacity that attracted me, and I hoped someday we would connect on a deeper level. Any woman who could run an organization with such an emotional and intense scope and raise two daughters was a woman I wanted to know. Never would I have predicted how our lives would intersect nor the depth that our professional and personal lives would go.

Overall, the concept of therapy gave me a case of the heebie-jeebies. When I had insomnia as a teenager, my parents took me to a counselor. He asked me questions like, "Do you love yourself? Has any adult ever touched you inappropriately?"

I threw up walls, strengthened my inner fortress, and refused to ever submit to such a vulnerable experience with a stranger again.

When Betsey handed me Hilary's contact info, I rubbed up against my itchy resistance to this type of counseling.

"I've actually thought about quitting my job just so she could be available to me as a therapist." Betsey went on, "Because Hilary's on staff here at DOVE, it would be a conflict of interest for her to take any of us on as clients. But I know I'm not alone in feeling this. She's that damn good, Julia."

Betsey didn't mince words, so I set aside my trep-idation and called for an appointment. Truthfully, I had to meet this woman who embodied such wisdom and greatness.

I met Hilary at her office, which was a sweet little cabin near the water. I appreciated the privacy it offered, given the small-town propensity for everyone being in each other's business. She greeted me warmly at the door. Inside, I saw a cozy red blanket spread on a couch awaiting me.

"I've been very excited to meet you, Julia. Everyone at DOVE speaks so wonderfully of you." Hilary sat in a leather chair and gestured toward the couch. I took the blanket and secured it like a seat belt across my lap.

"Before we begin, I want you to know that I am deeply sorry and angered that you experienced such a violent betrayal in our community. You did not deserve any of what happened to you."

"Thank you, Hilary. I refuse to let this horrible experience strip me of my love of people. That's why I'm here. I'm here to rebuild love in my heart."

Clutching my chest, I looked Hilary in the eye. "I want my story to be the one where love wins. And I want people to know my story."

"I see this for you, Julia. I am fully committed to support you in all aspects of your healing journey. Are you ready to begin?"

Throughout my first weeks of meeting with Hilary, I learned a profoundly transformative approach to healing that I added to my toolbox. Hilary taught me that pain lives on in our nervous systems even after our bodies have physically healed. Talking about experiences of trauma is not enough to truly liberate ourselves from ongoing anxiety and suffering. By applying a powerful psychotherapy technique called EMDR (Eye Movement Desensitization and Reprocessing), Hilary helped me release the stored energy of pain from the assault and clear out space for health to rebuild in both my mind and body simultaneously.

I realized during my initial sessions with her that there are people trained as therapists and there are people who are born healers. Hilary was my healer. She gifted me deep reassurance that all hearts can mend and regrow from trauma and become whole over time using the tools and strategies she empowered me with.

Even though I couldn't imagine a complete pathway out of pain just yet, I could trust that there was a well-lit way forward and that I wouldn't have to walk that road alone.

19. NO JUSTICE, NO PEACE?

One of the most vital ways we sustain ourselves is by building communities of resistance, places where we know we are not alone.

– bell hooks

"Julia, you deserve your day in court standing in your truth. But I can't advise going forth and bringing your case to trial. The odds are firmly against you in even having a judge accept your case."

When Jess, my whip-smart lawyer, uttered these words, my stomach landed in my shoes. She had done everything in her power to put together the puzzle pieces of my night of darkness, but it wasn't enough. The darkness won, and the district prosecutor wouldn't take my case.

Little precedence existed for courts taking cases involving date-rape drugs because the victims had little or no memory of the events that had occurred and, therefore, no memory of expressing consent or not. Even with DNA evidence, like I had, and the test results showing Rohypnol in my system, there was a less than a 5 percent chance of a court picking up my case.

What does one do after being hurt so badly with no hope of anyone being held accountable? I did the only thing I could do. I left the office and screamed bloody murder in my car. Rage poured from my lungs like a soul trapped in hell. The nearby dentist office must have been terrified. I just sat there screaming until I was empty.

The next morning, I awoke to an email from Betsey. She wanted to meet with Amanda and me ASAP regarding an idea she had. I wanted anything positive that I could hold onto. When I arrived at Open Space, Amanda was waiting in her car.

"How are you doing, honey? I've been thinking about you all morning." Amanda was my emotional anchor, and between her and Betsey, I knew whatever came forth from this meeting would be the best solution possible in the moment.

"I'm hanging on by a thread. But I'm excited to hear what Betsey is conjuring up."

"Me too. Our justice system is just fucked upside down. But I know that this meeting will bring about some good in the world. It has to."

We entered DOVE. I took a deep breath and walked into Betsey's office.

"Julia, first off, I want you to know I'm pissed as hell that you won't have the day in court that you deserve. I've been so angry ever since Jess told me she can't bring your case to trial. Everyone at DOVE is upset about this injustice."

Amanda and Betsey both put their hands on my shoulders. They were literally holding me together.

"I was awake all night," Betsey said, "and at about 3 this morning, an idea came to me. Are you OK with me sharing this now? Because I'm happy to spend our time however you need, Julia."

"Yes, please share with me. I really need some hope in my heart right now."

"Absolutely. I came up with a new prevention program that DOVE can sponsor. It's called Vashon SAFE, which stands for Sexual Assault Free Establishments. It will function as an educational training for restaurant owners and employees about drugs and alcohol relative to sexual assault."

Amanda took some notes. It was a lot to take in.

Betsey continued, "The idea is to empower bartenders and servers with information about what do in the event that someone is drugged or overly intoxicated, and therefore more susceptible to sexual assault. Also, it will help bars create a protocol that prevents drinks from being drugged in the first place."

Thoughts flashed through my mind. "Betsey, you are definitely onto something here. How can I be a part of this?" I caught eyes with Amanda, and she nodded.

"Are you still doing the newspaper article?" she asked.

A reporter from our local paper had approached me for an interview. News of what happened had traveled fast, fueled by social media and grocery store gossip. I was terrified to become the poster-child "Victim of Vashon."

I was worried my kids would read the article or have people talk to them about it, since they only knew a version of what had happened to me. But my fears didn't outweigh my desire to help others. I knew that there were women in my own community sitting alone in their silence, in their feelings of shame, and in their pain.

"Yes, I scheduled the interview this Friday." I took a deep breath then added my own idea, "I want this program to roll out at the same time as the article drops. I want my interview and the description of Vashon SAFE to be side by side on the front cover. Can you help get that to the newspaper, Betsey?"

"You know it." Betsey started jotting down a timeline on the whiteboard.

Amanda said, "I definitely want Open Space to be the first establishment certified through the Vashon SAFE training."

Like three knights of the round table, we planned our strategy to get Vashon SAFE running and out to area bars as quickly as possible.

Amanda and I were getting ready to leave DOVE when Betsey interjected, "It will be interesting to see which places sign up for the training and which don't."

"I want to go with you to The Bike when you offer it to them, OK, Betsey?" The Bike was where I had been drugged, and they also had a reputation for over-serving patrons.

"You bet. Amanda, do you want to come?"

"Only if I get to scare the shit out of the manager."

Walking into The Bike sent chills down my spine. Amanda witnessed my tensing and reached for my hand.

"Is Richard in?" Betsey asked the bartender for the general manager.

I'd met him before. He seemed easygoing and pleasant enough. After a minute or so, he appeared from a back office.

"Hello, there. I'm Betsey from The DOVE Project. I'm sure you've read the article of what happened to Julia a few months ago."

Richard interrupted, "Yeah, I'm really pissed about it all, to be honest. It's really not fair to blame the bar for getting fucked up."

Everyone's posture straightened. He continued, "No one has ever claimed to have been drugged here before, and I know that women lie about stuff like that because they are loose and get drunk and want to blame someone else for what happens to them."

Richard looked right at me. My blood boiled. I glanced at Amanda and was glad she wasn't armed.

"Richard, you're a fucking idiot," Amanda stated emphatically. "I will make damn sure that no woman EVER walks into this place again. You're lucky that I left my—"

Betsey placed herself between Amanda and Richard and finished her pitch.

"Look, Richard, the reality is that Julia was drugged here and nearly died as a result," Betsey affirmed. "There's proof, so it's not up to you whether you want to believe it or not. The community wants answers and needs safe places to eat and drink. If you don't value that, then so be it, but Vashon will not support you."

We marched out of the bar.

"What a motherfucking fool. I was so close to killing him with my bare hands." Amanda boiled.

Betsey kept silent. I was dumbstruck by Richard's vile ignorance. But I knew he wasn't the only one. There was a lot of work to be done.

Amanda and I in "No More" campaign poster distributed through DOVE and Vashon SAFE, addressing the intersection between alcohol, drugs, and sexual violence, 2017.

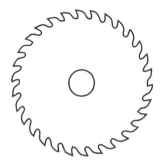

TROLL DOLLS

Remember those wacky troll dolls that first became popular in the 1960s? I had 83 of them in fifth grade, and one day I brought my favorite dolls to school to show the class. As a passionate collector, each one had a name, and I adored them like they were my special little buddies. At recess, I placed them carefully in the back of my desk and went out to play. When the bell rang, I rushed inside and witnessed a horrible massacre. My sweet trolls were strewn about on the dirty floor beneath my desk with colorful chunks of hair cut from their heads. Like a medic on a battlefield, I swept each one into my arms and assessed the damage.

Everyone was returning to their seats from recess, and the teacher approached the board to begin math instruction. I, one of the most law-abiding kids in grade school, remained in shock on the ground holding my fallen friends.

"Julia, return to your seat please."

Obediently, I rose. Holding them all wrapped in my skirt, I shuffled back to my seat. Looking around for answers, I spotted Andy with a smug look of satisfaction on his face. He smiled an evil smile. Oh, how I hated him in that moment. Pure, raw hate. But I refused to let him know. I refused to let him have the pleasure of my pain.

I turned back toward the teacher. Tears welling in my eyes, I stuck my head in my desk and started counting: 1, 2, 3... I pretended to look for a pencil or something else required for mathematics. Once I gained composure, I came out holding a ruler. I turned back to Andy and gave him the shoot-out stare. Something assured me that a higher power would take care of this injustice and I needn't worry. I just had to trust that what goes around comes around...and then start making some troll hats.

20. THE CONFRONTATION

I love to see a young girl go out and grab the world by the lapels. Life's a bitch. You've got to go out and kick ass.

– Maya Angelou

He was standing behind the dirty window, drinking a beer with a pool stick in his hand. While strolling through town after dinner with Craig, I looked in the window of the bar where I had been drugged. The place where I had sipped from the poisoned glass as innocently as Snow White. I couldn't pass by without peering in that hole, hungry for a clue to solve the mystery of the darkness that still held me.

And, bam! There he was. He just stood there, unaware that I had identified him as the man in bed next to me when I awoke from the abyss. He was the stranger in his early 20s who had violently attacked my body, my heart, my spirit.

"Craig, he's in there. Oh fuck, he's right there in the bar. Look!"

Craig cocked his neck sharply.

"Where, that kid at the pool table?"

"Yes. Yes! Oh, yes. He's right in there. We're going in."

Craig shot me a look like a buck in the headlights with the front bumper against his chest. "No. Julia. No, we really shouldn't…"

I grabbed his hand midsentence and swept the door open grandly, a gunslinger eager for a showdown. Craig was behind me, still in shock. The bar, bursting with drunken conversation, fell silent.

Everyone looked at me. He looked at me. The blackness in his eyes widened as I walked over to him. I could have struck him dead. But instead, I spoke.

"You. It's YOU!"

He stepped back in retreat. I watched the bartender grow tense, recognizing he may need to intervene.

In this moment of reckoning, when I felt invincible because of the rage that pulsed through my blood, I took a deep breath. Every warrior woman, goddess, and mother lifted me into a place of action based on my truth.

"Hey, everyone. This son of a bitch right here, he hurt me. He fucking stole me from my family, beat me up, and raped me. My kids thought I was dead because I just went and disappeared one night. And he doesn't even know my fucking name."

I pierced him with my diamond stare then screamed, "WHY? Why? Answer me, you piece of shit, why did you do this to me?" I pointed at him as if the tip of my finger was loaded.

Craig came closer, waiting expectantly for something bad to happen. I could feel Craig's anxiety but didn't allow it to penetrate my need to be heard. The young man cowered and said nothing. His eyes fell to the floor. No one reacted. Even though many of the faces in the bar were familiar to me, no one moved in support or in retaliation. No one offered me recognition, an explanation, or an apology.

As I stood there expectantly, the gravity of justice slapped me—I didn't need the why. I had my own story, my own strength, and my own way of recovery. No one outside of me was going to rescue me. No amount of punishment for this man-child would make my heart healed. So, I turned and walked out.

When I hit the pavement outside the bar, I wasn't the same woman who had walked in. I had faced my villain, and he was nothing more than a broken young man. I had stood before him and now on the sidewalk of my hometown as the hero of my own story. I had rescued myself from being a voiceless victim. In fact, I had just pinned myself with the wings of justice. And now it was time to fly.

With the article about my assault out, the program launched, and island restaurants and bars signing up for Vashon SAFE training, I started to feel my first inklings of stability. People began sharing their own stories with me about being drugged, many of them not knowing what had happened until reading my interview in the paper. A man told me he went into The Bike for a beer after work and passed out between two parked cars. A woman shared that she went in for a cocktail and had to call her husband to come get her because she was so messed up. I was shocked how common it was for people to feel or know they had been drugged in bars, especially on a small rural island.

After a while, people started boycotting The Bike and posting on social media that island residents should put their money where their values were. Local musicians stopped playing in bars without Vashon SAFE certification.

I heard occasional whispers from nonbelievers, but mostly I experienced a huge outpouring of concern, support, and care. I was asked to speak before the Rotary and share my story, along with an overview of the Vashon SAFE training. When DOVE had their annual fund-raising campaign, I was the guest speaker and helped raise much-needed funds for victims of violence. Though I will never have my day in court, I will always have my truth. By sharing my story, I not only help myself transform from victim to antiviolence activist, but I also support others in navigating their way out of the darkness of trauma. Being a promoter of healing and love is the best justice served. Period.

One day when I was picking up my son from school, a friend came running up to my car.

"Julia! Julia! Guess what?"

"Oh my gosh, tell me!"

"The Bike closed down. Hopefully forever! Look, it's in the paper!"

She handed me the newspaper open to the page: *The Bike Closes its Doors*.

"Thank fucking God. I will finally be able to sleep better knowing that no one else will ever be hurt in there. Halle-fucking-lujah!"

I called Amanda right away, and we shrieked together with victorious joy.

"I hope Richard goes back to the rock he crawled out from under," I shouted.

"That dickhead. He better hope he never runs into me on a dark sidewalk," Amanda replied.

"I wouldn't wish that on anyone, Amanda. Not even my worst enemy."

21. THE RIDGE BEAM

Don't be afraid of your fears. They're not there to scare you. They're there to let you know something is worth it.

– C. JoyBell C.

The ridge beam to a house is like a backbone to a blue whale. It holds the whole damn thing together. This thick piece of wood spans from one end of the house to the other and supports the rafters, which distribute the load from the roof.

The day my beautiful beam was set into place at my house was like receiving the best chiropractic healing. Seeing the giant staff of wood dangling off a crane, waiting to be caught and attached to the frame, was a perfect visualization of how I was resetting my own emotional backbone. It took many steady and trusted hands to facilitate my reconstruction as well as my own desire to persevere through the pain. Looking up at the mighty beam, I felt my own core strength and smiled.

Placing a ridge beam is like a well-choreographed tightrope act. Not only does it take brute strength and agility to balance at the top of a ladder while simultaneously directing the placement of an extremely heavy beam into place, but it must be done with another person doing everything in tandem on the opposite end. Needless to say, I wasn't the one on the ladder, but I did watch the whole thing, holding my breath; I misplaced a few years of my life worrying about the outcome given it was Don and Craig performing the choreography.

Once it was set and nailed off, we took a moment to admire this glorious sight, all of us standing securely on the earth looking up.

"You know what I like about the day the beam gets set?" Don wore a look of pride as he wiped sweat from his brow.

"When it's done and you're not dead?" Craig was struggling to pull a large splinter from his palm.

"Yes, I don't think anything scares me more than being that high on a ladder trying to grab a giant log swinging freely from a rope." Don took a long sip of water. "But once it's up there, then we can get the rafters up and dry the place in. That's what makes it a home—once it's got a roof and walls in place. The risk is always worth it."

I took a deep breath and looked at Craig and Don.

"There have been so many times when I've been scared shitless this past year. Watching you both up there reminded me of how healing works: you have to have courage to show up and construct yourself; to rebuild your infrastructure after you've been leveled. It's messy and hard. And fucking scary. You can't do it alone, but no one can do it for you. It requires a lot of grit and trust in yourself and others."

"You're one of the bravest people I know, Julia," Craig said. "When I was up there feeling my asshole pucker, I thought of how you keep going, how you keep loving even though you could hate everyone after what happened to you." Craig took a drag off his smoke and shot me a look of earnest adoration.

"Thank you for supporting me as I find myself again. For risking your lives to help build my dream. I love you both so much."

"Don't think we go around doing this for just anyone, OK, girl?" Don giggled.

"Deal. I can't wait to get the roof on, you guys, and get this baby dried in! I am ready to come home."

22. TEEN TRIUMPH

Dare to dream! If you did not have the capability to make your wildest wishes come true, your mind would not have the capacity to conjure such ideas in the first place.

– Anthon St. Maarten

As my heart was healing, I wanted to address one big, unresolved issue: launching the teen program at Open Space. After several months of fundraising and planning with Amanda, it was time to honor the requests and desires of that incredible group of young people I had worked with at the middle school. They represented the dreams and voices of so many kids on this island who hadn't been heard. I contacted their new teacher and asked to speak to the class about our upcoming event.

"Hey Ms. A., where the heck you been?" A young man shot me a big awkward smile. I barely recognized him with his newly grown facial hair and several inches added to his stature.

"Jorge! I have awesome news! I've been working at O Space turning your ideas into real opportunities for teens. We're about to launch our first event, and I wanted to tell you guys in person."

He had to think for a moment. Then it clicked.

"Wait, no way! It's happening? Like the stuff in our letters?"

"Yes! We're throwing a special night for teens only. I'll tell you all about it in just a moment. I'm here today to tell your whole class."

We walked in together. I saw many familiar faces. This was the high school version of my class for English language learners. I scanned to see who was present and, more significantly, to spot who wasn't. The dropout rate for native Spanish speakers in our district was appalling. I realized quickly that about half of my original students were missing. They would never know the impact of their letters, which twisted my gut sideways.

The bell rang. Within seconds, I stood before the kids holding tight to a myriad of emotions.

"Some of you may remember me from last year. I'm Ms. A., and I had the privilege of being your teacher. Together, we wrote letters to Open Space with your ideas for activities that would help teens on island."

Flickers of remembrance passed over their faces.

"I'm here to tell you that each of you have made a huge difference. Because of your ideas, we are launching a teen-only event in two weeks at O Space. There will be a band of high school kids performing, a DJ spinning music, loads of free food donated by your favorite restaurants, a visual artist doing spray art, and spaces that you can just hang out in with your friends."

Side conversations grabbed hold.

"Will parents have to come?"

"Nope, no parents allowed. There will be O Space employees keeping the vibe high and helping out if needed."

"How late will it go?"

"Until eleven."

More banter erupted.

"So, what ages of kids can come then?"

"13 to 16."

"Ms. A., we gotta get the word out. This is free, right? Do you have flyers with you? We gotta throw it up on our Snapchats and Instas."

"Yes, please, I need your help! This is your event, and I would love it if you all came and invited your friends. I don't even know what Snapchat is, so you all will have to work on that for me."

"It's all free, for reals? Even the food?"

"Yep. There will be endless platters of fresh-cooked food and tons of amazing desserts that have all been donated—100 percent free."

Jorge raised his hand. "Is there gonna be that water slide I wanted?"

"Not yet, but we've been talking about it for this summer."

He hooted, laughed, and high-fived another student.

When I returned to my car in the high school parking lot, I sat with all the feels. I relived the joy of those kids who for the first time felt that they mattered and could make a difference. I thought about the kids who were missing. Were they OK? Would their voices be buried forever in the shadows?

The event turned out nothing short of opening night on Broadway. It had taken all day to set the stage and sound for the band and DJ. Great care was taken to curate all the food that had been donated from several island restaurants and bakeries. A crew was dedicated to organizing the space to make it feel like a cool living room you'd see on MTV, yet also manageable for maintaining safety. The concept was to make it exactly as the kids had envisioned, with a sprinkle of adult oversight.

When the doors opened, one of my former students was the first to enter with her friend. They had never been to O Space and held the expressions of two children walking through the gates at Disneyland. Beelining to the buffet table, they giggled in awe. We'd made it look like something you'd see on a cruise ship.

"Dude, I've never seen this many blueberries in my life. I can't believe this. Shit, I've never even tried one before." This teenage girl had never experienced the beauty of a blueberry. My privilege blinders were blown off my face.

"My mom says they cost way too much, so I don't even ask if we can get them. But I've always wanted to try one since I was little."

I watched her take two or three into her hand, study them, and then pop them in her mouth. Upon the explosion of sweet nectar, her face blossomed with joy.

"May I take some more?"

"Guess what? I have a whole carton down here under the table, and they're all yours."

I handed her the bounty of berries, and she and her friend were overwhelmed with delight.

"There's more where these came from too."

Following the girls, a steady flow of teens arrived, many of whom had never been to an arts or music event on the island. Those experiences were reserved for families with money, the families who sent their kids to college and could speak English. But here were the unseen kids in our community, entering a wonderland that was of their own making.

Music filled the hall, and teens stenciled messages of their generations' triumphs and struggles on a large wall mural. Groups of young men and women danced together, laughed, and were treated like royalty.

Minutes from closing down, a kid came up to me whom I had never met.

"Hey, I just wanted to say that this was really cool. Thanks for not being a lame old person."

We both chuckled. "That's the best compliment I've had in a while. Take care, and I look forward to seeing you soon."

Teen Club O, 2018.

23. COMING HOME

You will know you have found your home when both your physical environment and energetic surroundings are in harmony with the individual you are within.

– DailyOM.com

I lit a beeswax candle that sat in the center of a delicious charcuterie board. As I watched the flame take to the wick, I imagined the bright smiles of my friends passing through the front door into my house for the first time to celebrate winter solstice. The interior was still unfinished, but the space felt warm with the woodstove ablaze and the Christmas tree lit in the corner. Every single piece of my house had been constructed with love—by love, for love— and now I was enveloped in it. I was love. I was standing inside my home, and home lived inside me as well.

A car pulled into the driveway. I popped a slice of salami into my mouth and ran to the door like a child expecting a present. I couldn't wait to experience the space filled with the precious people who inspired every action that lifted the walls surrounding me. It was Jake dropping off the kids. Dockton ran up the porch steps and into my arms.

"Mama, Mama, do we get to move in today?"

"Not quite yet, baby. We have to finish a few last things before it's ready. But we are having our first party today to celebrate the return of light after the darkness of winter."

Mirabelle stepped cautiously inside. "Mom, which room will be mine?"

"That one right upstairs. It will look out over beautiful blooming currants and foxglove in the springtime."

She slowly crept up the stairs and peeked into her new bedroom. I saw a little grin appear on her face. Calling down, she said, "Did you build my room, Mom?"

"Not just me, we all built it together—Craig, Don, and I. But I definitely pictured you and your brother playing and sleeping in your rooms when we framed up the—"

"Mama!" Dockton interjected, "Mama, you are my mama builder. I want to build big, big things with you."

"Yes, I want to build so many memories with you and your sister here. We can create anything we want, and we will make such great things together."

"Just as long as we never have to move out of here, OK?" Mirabelle came back down and grabbed a handful of crackers and cheese.

"Deal."

As my house swelled with loved ones, I cradled this monumental moment like a newborn lamb. Two years had passed since I had set sail, away from the security I had known, toward a new uncharted life. I had weathered many storms and been lost at sea more than once. But here I was, standing in the center of love that I had constructed with my own hands, with the loving help and guidance of my best friends. Home is where the heart is, and my heart was home.

Being under construction is a never-ending process of developing, demoing, rewiring, and adapting. That is what I know my life to be now—one hell of a brilliant, creative mess unfolding.

Mirabelle pulled me aside and said tenderly, "Thanks for building us a house. I know it wasn't easy. But you did it anyway."

"I had a dream, Mirabelle, and it is built now because of love. No matter what happens to us, in the end, love always wins."

My house under construction, winter solstice 2016.

I am a survivor. A builder. An advocate. A mother. A lover and friend. I am human. I am now and will forever be *Under Construction*.

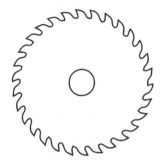

WISDOM
AND FOLLY

Brisk winter sunshine speckled the corner of my property past the garden near the road. As I walked toward a patch of sun in the yard, a flicker of movement caught my eye. A loose dog? No, it was a coyote running in my direction, then it stopped just across the street. We were within 30 feet of each other. The coyote stared at me and I back at it. I felt a deep and unexplainable connection to this spontaneously appearing canine.

Coyotes get a bad rap, but to me, they exhibit amazingly adaptive behaviors, able to survive, change, move, shift, outrun, and outthink most of their predators. This one seemed as if something had spooked it and it was uncertain about what to do, so it just stood there. Then suddenly, it started walking toward me, acting tame, as though it were a family pet. I stood frozen until it was only 15 feet from me, looking at me and still coming closer.

Instinct compelled me to run back to the fenced garden where I could have a boundary of protection. When I turned back around, it had retreated to the shadows across the road, but it was still looking at me. Straight through me. I admired its grace and thought about how it was known as The Trickster, an intelligent creator and keeper of magic, the balancer of wisdom and folly that go together. I thought about my follies and the wisdom that I hold because of them.

It turned and went deeper into the woods. I didn't want it to go away. I wondered what might have happened if I'd stayed calm and let it come to me. I thought of the paradox each of us lives with, yearning for adventure versus being safe and cautious, how desires and self-preservation battle each other from the moment we are aware of ourselves and others in the world.

We aren't born to overcome or escape fear. Why would we want to divorce an emotion intended for our very survival? Fear is not an enemy. It's like our first-grade teacher who told us to walk not run in the hall so we didn't bust our teeth on the tile floor. Our work with fear is to act as our own alchemist, to transmute it from disablement to informed excitement. To remove the veil of separateness that keeps us from sharing a common language.

At that moment, with the coyote, I was thrilled but had to run because my primitive brain kicked in and recognized the situation as possible danger. But in the eyes of the coyote, all I saw were compassion and acknowledgment. A messenger of love and oneness. We were both wild animals on opposite sides of the road in a chance meeting.

I stared into the darkness of dense forest across the road, wondering if he could still see me, why he had come to me. I shut my eyes and imagined my hands stroking the thick fur of his back. I hoped the coyote would come home to me some day. I knew next time, I wouldn't run away.

HEARTFELT ACKNOWLEDGMENTS

Eight months ago, the words to this story were locked deep in the corridors of my mind. Experiencing trauma does that: it disconnects us from our creativity, from our self-expression. Thanks to an incredible team of builder buddies, coaches, cheerleaders, and dearest family, I was able to recover my voice and release my narrative of constructing healing and hope—for myself and in the world.

To my children, Dockton and Mirabelle, who inspired me to take the risk to write this, you have taught me over and over that love conquers fear. To be a fierce champion of love in the world, even if the bad guy is on top. I cherish your belief in good and am forever grateful for your belief in me.

Thank you, Dad, for being a constant companion, my personal lighthouse, through all the storms. Your patience and support helped me persevere as I recovered and reclaimed myself. I love and appreciate all you've done for me, even when I haven't had the words to say so.

Donald and Craig, thank you for never letting me doubt for one second that I should share my truth. When I couldn't picture the darkness ending, you lifted me up into the sky where I could feel the sun on my face. Together, we built a beautiful nest for my family with sweat, tears, love, and a ton of laughter. You've taught me that humor heals all wounds and that inappropriate jokes are some of the best medicine out there.

I hold deep appreciation for my incredible tribe of women who have held and nurtured me while under construction: Vicki Sue, my incredible mother; Hilary, my healer; Cheryl Roberts Oliver, my wordsmith; Daniela, my spirit guide; Amanda, my ferocious big sister; Asia, my dearest soulmate; Jessica, my poker—I mean, talented acupuncturist.

Thank you to my dream team of advocates at The DOVE Project, who helped me have access to the tools needed for emotional remolding after being demoed. And for being a safe harbor when I needed to be held in uncertainty.

To Janet, David, and the visionaries at Open Space: you listened and responded to the teens of Vashon with art, heart, and soul and created an authentic space for them to explore, to create, and to dream. I appreciate each of you and the brilliant young people who entrusted me with their hopes and visions.

Huge waves of gratitude to the Davis Creative team. You've made self-publishing fun!

And to my crazy-ass friend Nate, I knew you were special when you made our teacher cry in our first week of second grade. Without you, I never would have found Don and my way into building. Thank you for only calling me half nuts for wanting to be a carpenter lady and for showing me that if you don't go out and ask for what you want, you won't get shit in this life.

INTERVIEW WITH "DREAM-BUILDER" DON ROBERTS

Julia: When we met at the Hardware Store Restaurant (isn't that funny that I met Don at a restaurant named "the Hardware Store"?!), what on earth were you thinking hiring me, a woman with zero experience in construction?

Don: I could tell you were smart right away. OK, and you were pretty too, but it was the fact that you could articulate what you wanted so clearly that I knew you could quickly learn construction. I love teaching people about my passion, and women do amazing as carpenters. Sure, physically there might be some limitations, but women pay close attention to detail. The best tilers, painters, and finish carpenters I've known have been women. And they bring such amazing energy to a crew. If I could, I'd only work with women and hire out some subcontractors to do the grunt work. You know, I think it's because I'm part woman [said with a giggle] or that I love women so much. Or both.

And I am so glad I hired you. Look at all you've brought to my business. How much more money we've made because of you taking over the books, bringing us great new clients, and because of building your house. Look at all you've brought to my life. Susy [Don's wife] and I love you to pieces.

J: What do you love most about building? Like, why, even at 65 years old, are you still doing this hard, physical work?

D: Wait, I'm 65 years old?! I feel like I'm 23. My parents didn't have a lot of money, and they didn't hand me a silver spoon. I had to make it for myself, so I did. I have had so many jobs, starting at a very young age. I almost became an architect, but my stepdad taught me the pride of working with my hands. I used to do concrete work with him in the desert and I loved it. I didn't mind sweating or hurting at the end of the day. Once I started building houses, I realized I wasn't just physically making things happen, I was making people's dreams happen. And that's when I fell in love with what I am doing. That's why I'm out here as an old guy still working away. Because I'm a dream builder. I can drive around the island looking at houses I've built and say, "Look, I built that dream, and that dream." And who wants to retire from that? Not me. Not ever.

J: If you could give any advice to a person like me who felt like she could never be a builder, what would you tell her about following her passion?

D: I'd tell her to fucking go for it. We are all gonna die, and it doesn't hurt to ask. We don't feel like we have permission to get what we really want, but we do. You've always told me that you almost didn't ask me if I'd hire you that day at the restaurant. What if you hadn't? You would be miserable. You wouldn't have your home. You'd still be broke. But you did ask, and it all came together. I'd tell that person, "Hey, go have a glass of wine and pitch your idea to the person sitting next to you at the bar. See what happens. Believe in yourself."

But I'd also tell that person, "Do your research." Not everyone can be a good teacher. I love helping people learn construction, but there are 10 other contractors that would hate that, having a person asking questions, needing support. Find the right people to help you up in life. They are out there. And don't get discouraged if at first you don't find your teacher. Keep trying. Try a new bar [said laughing]. Give yourself permission to be happy.

ABOUT THE AUTHOR

Julia Harriet is a dreamer and a silly heart. She is also a builder and a survivor. As the mother of two incredible children, she loves to play, learn, and love.

After spending a decade teaching everything from preschool to high school art, she followed her heart that dreamed to one day build her own home and began a carpentry apprenticeship. Julia's been working in construction ever since and imagines her life to always be a project under construction.

Made in the USA
Monee, IL
29 January 2022